CORPORATE BRAVERY

CORPORATE BRAVERY

ELIMINATE FEAR-BASED
DECISION MAKING

ISBN: 978-0-692-49229-1

TABLE OF CONTENTS

SYNOPSIS

AMERICAN CULTURE HAS become a culture of fear. Parenting methods and advertising messages scream for safety. Terrorism's threat and the government's response both tell us to take cover. And, of course, social media's unending streams perpetually magnify it all.

In this societal context, our business cultures, too, have become cultures of fear. Mistrust is rising between management and co-workers, all seeking to protect personal interests. Advisors push us toward fear-based caution, not opportunity-seeking strategy. External influences — from the media to regulators to competition — focus us on avoiding risks rather than moving boldly ahead.

Corporate Bravery is a book about freeing your business from being a culture of fear. It starts by considering fear's impact on decision-making. Then, it explores eight ways that fear can harm culture. Finally, through a three-step process, it shows how to foster a culture that supports engaged employees, provides opportunities for measured risk-taking and innovation, and rewards the brave leadership that drives business success.

ACKNOWLEDGEMENTS

THANK YOU TO my wife Peggy for giving me the freedom to step away from time to time from our family so that I could write my thoughts. You are an amazing wife and I truly appreciate our partnership.

Thank you to my editor, Chris Molnar, your mastery of writing concepts truly took this to a new level. Thanks for keeping me out of trouble with my High School English teachers.

Thank you to the coffee shop baristas that didn't kick me out of your shops while writing this book. Especially, after getting lost in my favorite tunes with my earphones in and likely distracting the rest of your patrons with my tapping to the beats.

Thank you to all my friends that encouraged me, provided feedback and otherwise didn't laugh at me for thinking I could be an author.

Finally, thank you to all the companies that I have worked at, with cultures good and bad, that have provided so much of the material for this book.

INTRODUCTION

MY WIFE SPENT her early childhood years moving around the country, so her mother home-schooled her, building her self-confidence and strength despite the frequent relocations. By the time she joined a public school in fourth grade, she was strong enough to not be battered about by teasing, popularity, or concerns about her role in group dynamics. She wasn't the most attractive girl or the most popular, but she courageously leaned into who she was.

As she continued to grow and mature through her college years, she blossomed into a woman who truly understood herself, held strong to her beliefs, and was ready to make an impact on the world. And, obviously, on me.

While Peggy brought a strong, self-confident — dare I say brave? — person to our marriage, I brought a handful of fears. I wasn't a ball of insecurities, but I definitely had my weak areas. At five, I was bitten badly by a Doberman. I grew up in poverty and lived off government assistance. Money fears were constant. Later, I chased visions of success that changed with each profile I read in business magazines, fearing I might not achieve any of them. Much of my life was built around fear.

We spent the first few years of our marriage establishing a culture that wasn't driven by fear. Early on, we created a family mission and values, which went a long way toward establishing how we were going to grow our family and the identity we wanted to create for our children. One of the value statements we added was the following:

> *Develop ourselves by choosing to challenge our limits.*
> We will avoid complacency and stagnation by
> always pushing past limits we have established for
> ourselves. "Search me, O God, and know my heart;
> test me and know my anxious thoughts. See if there
> is any offensive way in me, and lead me in the way
> everlasting." (Psalms 139:23-24)

It was on this foundation that we began to grow our family — first our son Peter, then the twins. We took pride in being a family that made decisions not out of fear but rather in alignment with our family mission and values. For example, we went on a mission trip to an orphanage in Mexico when Peter was 10 months old. Though it was at the height of the Mexican drug cartel wars that claimed the lives of tens of thousands (including many innocent bystanders), we felt it was an important experience for us at that moment. We weren't going to be deterred by our fears.

We still filter all our decisions through this lens of challenging our limits. It helps greatly to have a partner who challenges me beyond my own fears and asks what I don't always want to ask: "Are we making this decision in fear of a possible outcome, or are we making this decision because it is the best thing for us?"

I am fortunate to have someone ask those questions and work with me to establish a culture for our family. But, in a larger business or organization, a multitude of influences and voices can open up cracks for fear to creep in and affect decision-making. This is a book about stopping fear from driving outcomes that are not only non-optimal, but even bad for a business's long-term health. This is a book about seeking opportunity despite — or even because of — risk. This is a book about being brave.

The Whaleship Essex

After I made the commitment to start the journey of writing this book, I stumbled across a TED Talk from Karen Thompson, author of *The Age of Miracles*. Her talk centers on the story of the whaling ship *Essex*, which eventually became the basis for Herman Melville's classic novel *Moby Dick*. I was already familiar with *Moby Dick,* but the *Essex* still drew me in because it's simply a fascinating tale.

Digging in, I found Thomas Nickerson's first-hand account in Nathaniel Philbrick's book *In the Heart of the Sea: The Tragedy of the Whaleship* Essex. I devoured the book and realized it had a lot of real lessons for today's leadership and corporate environment — contemporary issues like fear-based decision-making or being paralyzed by anxiety.

For those unfamiliar with the story and its context, here's a quick version.

The whaling ship *Essex* was based out of Nantucket, Massachusetts, in the early 1800s. Nantucket during that time was the epicenter for whaling, much like Hollywood for today's movie industry. Long before oil rigs and deep sea drilling, whaling was the primary source for the oil that was used to light and heat homes. In addition, Nantucket was a Quaker community:

> One of the defining paradoxes of Nantucket's whalemen was that many of them were Quakers, a religious sect stoically dedicated to pacifism, at least when it came to the human race. Combining rigid self-control with an almost holy sense of mission.

> Nantucket's ever growing number of Quakers were hardly free-thinking individuals. Friends (as they were called) were expected to conform to rules of behavior determined during yearly meetings, encouraging a sense of community that was as carefully controlled as that of any New England society. Bedtime stories told of killing whales and eluding cannibals in the Pacific.

As a result, Nantucket was a community obsessed with omens and signs. A recent comet appearance and swarms of locusts in the turnip fields did nothing but bolster the feeling of dread within the community.

Yet Nantucket was also on its way to becoming one of the richest towns in America. The whaling industry was a booming industry in a world economy sunk in depression. In the absence of liquid capital markets, it was also a source of good returns for investors in the US, generating annual returns in the 30–40% range. These investors, always eager to increase their returns, pushed boats into ever-longer tours at sea. As Philbrick writes, "Owners were always reluctant to invest any more money in the repair of a ship than was absolutely necessary."

One of 70 whaling boats based in Nantucket, the *Essex* was no different. There could have been suspicious areas below the waterline that owners chose to address at a later time, if not ignore. This same attitude pervaded the provisioning of the ships as well:

> Gideon Folger and Paul Macy, two major shareholders in the *Essex*, were prominent members of the island's Quaker upper class. Yet, according to Nickerson, Macy, in charge of outfitting the *Essex* that summer of 1819, attempted to cut costs by severely under-provisioning the ship.

In addition to these risks, whaling itself was not a job for the faint of heart. These whale-hunting trips could last 2 or 3 years at a time, possibly including a round-trip journey from Nantucket, into the Atlantic, around the southern tip of South America, and deep into the Pacific. As for catching the whale:

> Harvesting sperm whales — the largest toothed whales in existence — was no easy matter. Six men would set out from the ship in a small boat, row up to their quarry, harpoon it, then attempt to stab it to death with a lance. The sixty-ton creature could destroy the whaleboat with a flick of its tail, throwing the men into the cold ocean water, often miles from the ship.

As the industry expanded, able crewmembers often found themselves in a rapid ascension from hand to captain after only a couple trips to sea. The *Essex*, before its fateful trip, had seen exactly such an ascent: its Captain George Pollard had recently been promoted. It was his first time captaining a whaling trip.

His trip was beset with multiple setbacks nearly from the start. The ship was capsized in the Atlantic by a storm. The crew started — and was nearly burned alive by — a forest fire on an island they stopped at for supplies. And that was before the famous large sperm whale destroyed their boat in the middle of the Pacific.

What followed next was a fight for survival on the high seas. The twenty men battled heat, lack of water and food, storms, and turbulent waves. In the end, eight survived. It was a tragedy on par with the *Titanic* for its generation, not only for its scale but also for how it captured the nation's attention.

Its application to our subject matter is the role fear played in decision-making by the townspeople, the ship's owners, and the ship's crew. Was the town afraid of losing its status, pressuring citizens to work where they weren't equipped? Were the owners afraid of losing profits, making them rush the ship to sea? Was the crew afraid of coming back empty-handed, pushing them to take reckless risks? Beyond any single decision, many small decisions can create a culture of fear and negatively influence our ability to make the best decision in a crucial, potentially life-threatening (or profit-maximizing) situation.

Leadership, management styles, team political environments, the role of investors, and competition — these and other factors will be explored in depth throughout this book along with some practical ways to rise above fear-based management and decision-making and become the bravest manager you can be.

Before we dive in, you can even start to ask yourself some questions from the *Essex*'s story:

1. What unique combination of factors in your corporate culture could lead you down a route that feels safe only because it's familiar?

2. Are you clinging to any broken and tattered whaling ships?

3. What imaginary fears might actually lead you into even greater dangers?

1
WHAT IS FEAR?

I WANTED TO START this book with a simple definition of fear, but we each have our own versions. Fear can be simple like snakes or roller coaster rides, yet it can morph into a debilitating neurosis preventing us from becoming the best person, spouse, parent, or leader that we could be.

A recurring fear I have is missing appointments, and I swear it's entirely rooted in being late for class on my first day of middle school. This experience — which made me feel so disappointed in myself — embedded itself into my subconscious and become deeper and darker over time. So much so that, by the time I was ready to graduate from college, I had recurring nightmares of missing an entire semester of Spanish class and not realizing it until the last week of the semester.

This may seem mostly benign. I *didn't* miss a semester of Spanish, after all. Basic definitions of fear even indicate that there is a strong survival quality in fear that is good and protective:

Fear is frequently related to the specific behaviors of escape and avoidance, whereas anxiety is the result of threats that are perceived to be uncontrollable or unavoidable. It is worth noting that fear almost always relates to future events, such as worsening of a situation, or continuation of a situation that is unacceptable. Fear can also be an instant reaction to something presently happening. All people have an instinctual response to potential danger, which is in fact important to the survival of all species.

While the anxiety of anticipating some future possible negative outcome can in fact be a protective human response, fear can be damaging over a long-time horizon.

Travis Bradberry, the co-author of *Emotional Intelligence 2.0* (the series famous for popularizing the EQ concept so popular among corporate trainers), put together this diagram

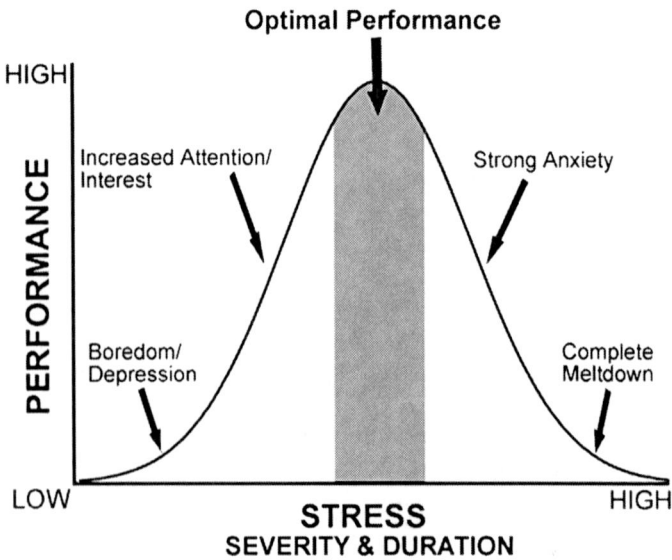

Studies have shown that some stress or concern for potential consequences can create higher or possibly even peak performance. However, if it is an ever-present hum in the background of life or comes in bursts that are too intense for the human emotion to handle it can in fact become debilitating.

I contend that this debilitating nature happens more and more not just in our personal lives, but increasingly in our organizations — whether they be large enterprises, start-up companies, mid-sized businesses, non-profits, sports teams, or even volunteer groups. We are constantly being conditioned to fear and protect against failures — which only serves to make us more afraid and less willing to take and seize opportunities.

GCL Davey, in his research study "A conditioning model of phobias," concluded that verbal threat information, by creating threat expectancies, increases the strength and speed with which we develop an association between a conditioned stimulus and a fear-evoking outcome.

For example, a child who believes that a dog will bite her and is subsequently bitten will have a stronger dog-trauma association than a child who didn't previously believe the dog would bite. The child who feared the dog thinks her beliefs have been confirmed. The child who did not fear the dog takes it as an anomaly. This very phenomenon was written about by Andy Field in his research paper "Verbal Information Pathway to Children's Fears." The clear discrepancy between the two groups can be seen in this chart — including how the fear-level persists over time.

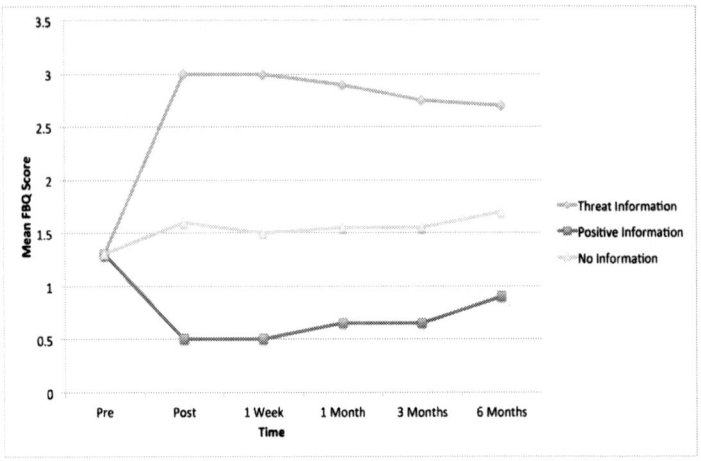

Let's translate this to business. Take an organization that is heavily risk-averse and always guarding against failure. When this organization does suffer a failure, the impacts on the culture can be more severe than at an organization that doesn't fear failure but rather views it as a natural learning process.

Understanding my Biases

I should provide background so you at least know my biases up front. For one, my wife Peggy and I are basically free-range parents — the antithesis of a helicopter parent. Someone who doesn't hover with a bottle of Purell at the playground or show up with a son at his job interviews. Rather, we provide so much space that many of the over-caffeinated, neurotic parents — or just regular people — in our community could construe our actions as neglectful.

When we go in public with our children (6-year-old son and 4-year-old twin girls), it is not uncommon to see the judgmental, condescending glances from other adults at our "obvious" disregard for our children's safety. Our friends openly mock our laissez faire attitude toward bumps, bruises, and cuts.

We justify this approach by extolling the virtues of those very bumps, bruises, and cuts as learning opportunities. One fall from a chair that splits a lip — which will happen anyway even under the eyes of the most attentive parent — will embed itself into a child's memory bank. They will then be much less likely to repeat that behavior than if they'd been whisked away by a mom or dad before they could attempt it. In fact, being removed from the environment without grasping the consequences only makes them want to try it that much more.

My wife likes to say that she wants them to discover consequences where and when they can do limited harm, then be more careful when they come into a truly dangerous situation.

Religious Backgrounds and Foundations

To those without religious backgrounds, it may seem counterintuitive to think that most major religions actually come against fear. Many people see fear used as a means for conversion. However, there is a difference between what a religion teaches and how its followers act it out. Keep in mind that what a religion teaches was generally written to believers at that time. Those who were reached by the message struggled with those things — and still struggle with them, because they are very human urges or impulses.

But, in general, religions do tend to come against fear. The

Bible contains 205 examples of people being afraid. But the consistent theme of Christianity is that fear has no place in everyday life and that God will protect His people. Genesis 1:28 says that we are to fill the earth and subdue it. To rule over every living creature he has created, not to be in submission to a fear of all of those things. 1 John 4:18 says there is no fear in love, but that perfect love casts out fear. For fear has to do with punishment, and whoever fears has not been perfected in love.

And, in a story from the book of Judges, God has his servant and army-commander Gideon send home two-thirds of his troops because they were fearful. While that put Gideon at a competitive disadvantage, it was necessary to avoid disrupting God's plan. The fearless troops won.

Fear is the opposite of trust, and trust is the essence of the relationship between Christ-followers and God. It is not that God says, "Don't fear," as much as that He says, "Go boldly." Fear ultimately prevents us from stepping out boldly into the best opportunities that may exist — whether personally or for an organization.

While my personal worldview is Christian, basic research on other religions reveals some consistent themes. Hindus believe that the soul can be reincarnated, undergoing a cycle of rebirth. Hindus believe that a soul is able to undergo numerous lifetimes within a physical body. All of the past lives that you have led contribute to the person you are today. Thus, Hindu tradition teaches not to fear death because life will continue in another physical body.

Buddhism addresses the self-generated type of fear. This is fear that comes out of a telling and retelling of our personal stories and fantasies. Buddhism would address this by seeing into your stories, realizing that fear is the mind working in overdrive. Meditation practice is described as one way to face fear and learn to deal with it.

In other words, fear is a topic that has been broached by religions from all cultures — and, in general, fought against.

Fear Responses

So we know that fear is a natural human response. That some fear can protect us from danger. And that most religions believe in bravery and not fear. But what does this mean? And what should we do when we experience fear?

In February 2013, *Reader's Digest* published an article entitled "How the Science of Fear Makes Soldiers Stronger." While the article's focus is primarily related to soldiers and the battlefield, it is a relevant regardless of situation. Neurobiologist Lilianne Mujica-Parodi, who has studied volunteers for years in stressful situations to identify how the brain reacts, talks about the fear response:

> "You don't want someone without a fear response at all. That's not brave; that's just abnormal. But a high stress response is also unhealthy." The optimal fear response, she says, accurately assesses risk, saves room for cognitive thought, and rapidly returns to baseline when the danger passes.

> "Fear is the enemy," says Comdr. Eric Potterat, PhD, a Navy SEALS Special Warfare group psychologist.

The mental stress of war has claimed more casualties in Iraq and Afghanistan than bombs and bullets.

"There are people who make a negative loop about the situation they are placed in," says Potterat. "Those are people who can't cope." It's the people who take control of stressful challenges "in any environment," he says, who will eventually wear the SEAL uniform.

The bottom line isn't whether we fear. It's how we respond to fearful situations. There are many ways we can respond to fearful situations. Extreme responses never end in a place that is healthy, either on an individual level or organizationally.

This book isn't about denying a very human emotion. Rather, it is about understanding the feelings, putting them in the right context, and ultimately responding with a clear mind.

In review, fear is natural and can spur us to greater performance. But there are limits; more fear isn't better. The natural responses to fear that can propel can also paralyze us, especially when we encounter a situation that evokes a memory of a time a fear came true. We can train ourselves to overcome fears, but we first have to recognize how fear plays a role in our behaviors. Then, we can condition our minds to respond in a rational — even successful — manner.

2
FEAR GRIPPING OUR SOCIETY

"When our fears are bounded we are prudent, cautious and thoughtful. When our fears are unbounded and overblown we are reckless and cowardly. Our longings and worries are both overblown because we have the capacity to manufacture the very commodity we are constantly chasing."

— Dan Gilbert, Harvard Psychologist

I N A TED Talk, astronaut Chris Hadfield tells a story about a spacewalk where his vision was completely obscured by something in his eye. What do you do if you're blinded in space? Hadfield, like all astronauts, had trained and trained and trained — not just for how the mission could go right, but for all the ways the mission could go wrong. He wasn't out there alone, and he and his spacewalk partner had practiced incapacitated crew rescue, so he knew whatever happened, they could deal with it. He didn't panic, and, after a while, his tears cleared whatever had been blocking his vision (which turned out to be the anti-fog used to keep the helmet visors clear).

This story and his entire talk underscores how preparation and a desire to hit fears head-on can help us overcome them. Back on earth, marketing guru and author of 17 best-sellers Seth Godin wrote a blog post that sums up the current human condition as it relates to how fear is ruling our everyday lives:

> We're losing our ability to engage with situations that might not have outcomes shiny enough or risk-free enough to belong in the palace. By insulating ourselves from perceived risk, from people and places that might not like us, appreciate us or guarantee us a smooth ride, we spend our days in a prison we've built for ourselves.
>
> Shiny, but hardly nurturing.
>
> So, we ban things from airplanes not because they are dangerous, but because they frighten us. We avoid writing, or sales calls, or inventing or performing or engaging not because we can't do it, but because it might not work. We don't interact with strange ideas, new cuisines or people who share different values because those interactions might make us uncomfortable…
>
> Funny looking tomatoes, people who don't look like us, interactions where we might not get a yes…

Growth is messy and dangerous. Life is messy and dangerous. When we insist on a guarantee, an ever-increasing standard in everything we measure and a Hollywood ending, we get none of those.

Terrorism, political extremism, and safety standards that attempt to eliminate any chance of injury are just a few of the ways that American society has gone off the rails with fear in our culture. These societal fears are not new but have rather ebbed and flowed over the decades.

In the 1930s, it was economic fear — the ability to feed your family and find a way to earn an income during the Great Depression. In the 40s and 50s, it was war and the scourge that was the Nazi party — exacerbated by the bombing of Pearl Harbor. Then it was the rise of communism and fear of a nuclear holocaust in our standoff against the Soviet Union.

But our current malaise feels different. Maybe it is a subtler yet broader assault on all aspects of our lives.

Let's take a walk through a typical day in my life — probably not too far from an average American's day — to see all the ways our sensibilities are assaulted with fears and concerns.

5:45 AM — The alarm wakes me from my sleep. Only interrupted twice by my children and their fears about shadows they saw during the night! I also went to sleep later than I had hoped because, last night, my wife saw a speck and was concerned it could have been a bed bug. After all, the local news bombards us with information about how Cincinnati is the bed bug capital of the country.

5:55 AM — On the way to the gym, I unlock the front door. Even though we live in a relatively safe community with little crime or violence, I am constantly forced to confront the fact that we only have a deadbolt lock on the door instead of a two-way home security system with a live voice to scare an intruder away.

6:10 AM — We play racquetball, interspersed with discussion about my lack of goggles versus my friend's knee and ankle braces.

7:10 AM — I am back home to prepare breakfast and get the kids ready for school. Our always-evolving discussion of health and nutrition comes to a head here daily. The sugary cereals that their grandparents purchase would always be our kids' choices, but that rots their teeth out and gives them diabetes, but they're okay occasionally, right? Should I be making a protein- and fat-heavy meal of scrambled eggs for my wife and I, or is the saturated fat going to bite us later in life? Instead of buying the eggs from the supermarket, should we be raising chickens to provide our own? Or at least buying them locally? What about the harmful chemicals that farms use to prevent salmonella?

8:30 AM — I am shuttling the kids to school. My 6-year-old hasn't had a booster shot, a choice that is possibly illegal in most, if not all, 50 states. Despite the fact that the entire route to school is less than 1.5 miles and all the roads are residential with 25 mph limits, I can't let any of them ride in the front passenger seat because of my car's airbags.

9:00 AM — I am now at work. Thanks in part to the bed bug scare, I ran out of time last night to prepare the report my boss had asked for, and I am concerned about his reaction. I scan the previous months' reports: our sales figures are down.

Considering our expansion aspirations, we need cash flow to continue to come in stronger each successive month.

I could go on, but I think you get the point. Three hours into my day, all areas of my life have been greeted by messages of fear.

This seems normal. There's a lot to fear, isn't there? Like terrorism — a nameless, faceless enemy that isn't easy to characterize, doesn't have a pattern, and can't be isolated or eradicated through technology or American military superiority. Violence in supposedly safe places, like schools and movie theaters. And never-ending reports of newly discovered diseases, newly discovered carcinogens, newly discovered new things to be afraid of.

All are major contemporary fears, but I think a more revealing hallmark isn't in the causes but in our responses. Previously, we persevered. We had the stamina to overcome. We were almost defiant. But now we react with hypersensitivity to what can go wrong and avoid potentially bad things — no matter how unlikely they are or how impractical our "solutions." Let's look at both.

Fear Defenses

First, our barriers. Literal ones. Take a look at this photo from *Bloomberg Business.*

At Wall Street it's not exactly the picture of unbridled American optimism that Wall Street once represented. In what should be a happy social setting — people gathered for coffee and conversation — the bright barricades say something else entirely.

A similar scene is playing out at important sites all over our country. Contrast that with important sites in Europe or Asia, which are often very approachable. I could walk up and touch Michelangelo's *David* (and did so) as recently as 2003, and, despite Vatican workers rushing us on, I could immerse myself in the beauty of the Sistine Chapel without feeling surrounded by a war zone.

The Bloomberg article describes the escalating use of barriers:

Lower Manhattan is turning into an armored security zone. Antiterrorist paraphernalia litter parts of nine square blocks, or at least a dozen acres — all to protect the New York Stock Exchange from attacks. Where Broadway opens to Wall Street, jaw-like truck barriers and a plastic-tent guard booth block the street. A fence squeezes pedestrians into one narrowed sidewalk. Very soon, the Police Department will finish a plan to cordon off the entire 16-acre World Trade Center site, adding lines of bollards and nine vehicle-screening zones that come with credential-presentation queues, guard booths and pairs of those bladelike barriers projecting out of the street.

Sadly, the appearance of safety is just that — an appearance. These areas are really no safer to an attack — think these barricades would have done much during the original attack? — but the appearance of safety makes policy makers and officials feel better about their work.

For a more personal example, let's look at my current home of Ft. Thomas, Kentucky. This community of 16,000 people situated just a few miles south of Cincinnati, Ohio, has a water pumping and treatment facility that supplies most of the Northern Kentucky region, an area of about 500,000 people.

One aspect of its infrastructure is a series of reservoirs located in the middle of town. Surrounded by a mile-long track, they used to be a focal point of community activity. It was common to see hundreds of walkers, runners, and bikers taking advantage of the scenery. It was located near restaurants and bars, and it added a little something to the area of town called the Midway District.

After 9/11 and the increasing safety precautions, the town closed the reservoirs to public access by erecting a tall metal fence around the water supply. The theory went that by creating a barrier around them it would prevent terrorists from trying to poison the community.

A well-meaning change, but the reality is that anyone interested in tainting the water supply can walk right up to the iron-barred fence and lob in chemicals. Meanwhile, the community has lost a civic treasure.

Jonathan Marvel, an architect brought in on these projects to try to make the security aspects more visually appealing, said about all these deterrents, "Security devices make us afraid of each other. With less obvious barriers, you get more security and less fear."

Not to pick on New York again — and the Bloomberg connection is in name only — but another example of this fear is Mayor Bloomberg's attempt to ban sparklers statewide. That's right, those small summer treats whose worst harm is singeing a few fingers, banned. A report on the mayor's office press release reads:

> Mayor Bloomberg will urge Gov. Cuomo to veto legislation that would legalize the sale of sparklers outside New York City, arguing that terrorists could resort to using even kiddie fireworks to ignite a bomb. And that's a risk not worth taking, City Hall officials said.

> "While this bill excludes New York City, legalizing

these devices everywhere else in the state would, as a practical matter, have the same effect in the five boroughs," Joseph Garba, the mayor's state legislative director, said in a memo. "A recent attempt to harm innocent lives provides a frightening example of how legally purchased… fireworks can cause dramatic harm and even kill." Garba cited the case of failed Times Square bomber Faisal Shahzad, who bought a package of legal M-88 from out of state to help ignite his dud bomb in 2010."

Sparklers?! Really?! Terrorists will find a way to kill and destroy even if we ban every possible instrument that can be used to perpetrate an attack. That press release is dripping with insecurity, showing that the mayor's leadership comes from reactive fear, not confidence in its purpose, vision, and values.

This sort of leadership has been noticed — and parodied — by entertainers. In 2013, the Lonely Island — a comedy group that came to fame on NBC's *Saturday Night Live* — did a music video that repurposes YOLO, the popular abbreviation for "You only live once." A term usually used to signify freedom and a carefree lifestyle, it was converted it to "You oughta look out." The video features the group shouting YOLO, amidst images and lyrics calling out common contemporary fears including bank failures, plane crashes, and even insects. Throughout the video, the group grows increasingly (and hilariously) paranoid about all the ways they can be harmed.

Which is all to say that, whatever is causing our fear these days, our typical reaction is to fear it all the more — even when we have supposed protections from leadership.

In our own reactions to fear, we can seek comfort in illogical ways because we fear more than we logically should. *USA Today* chronicled an interesting phenomenon in the weeks after the Sandy Hook tragedy:

> Parents anxious about their children's safety are boosting sales of armored backpacks in the wake of the Sandy Hook school massacre, manufacturers are reporting.

> "I can't go into exact sales numbers, but basically we tripled our sales volume of backpacks that we typically do in a month — in one week," Derek Williams, president of Salt Lake City-based Amendment II, told Mother Jones on Tuesday.

If you are one of the parents who purchased one of the backpacks, I apologize — but that is absurd. Are we seriously so gripped with fear that we would drop $300 to protect our children for such a remote possibility? For something that a small elementary student would possibly not even be able to retrieve in time to protect herself?

To understand the imbalance — and confusion — caused by fear, let's consider the probability that a child would need to use this item. Each day, 74 million total school children and 45 million elementary school children go to school. A typical school year includes 180 days of instruction on average. That is 13.3 billion opportunities for something to go wrong with a child in school and 8.1 billion for elementary only. In all those opportunities, there were three school shootings in 2012 — one elementary school — totaling 30 fatalities, including 20 elementary school students. In other words, about one every 400 million.

If you have three kids, there's a greater chance of winning the lottery 220 times than having one be a casualty in a school shooting — yet the specter of fear doesn't cause people to run out and get a few $2 Powerball tickets to buy their kids' life-long security. They buy a $300 armored backpack that might not do a thing.

Think armored backpacks are an anomalous example? A 2014 *Bloomberg Business* article — "The Bulletproof Classroom" — chronicles government programs funding millions of dollars of classroom defensive mechanisms like armored whiteboards. The article is relevant beyond niche products and any single type of fear:

> Such odd inspirations are bound to come up when fear rises and money is thrown at the problem. They also raise questions: If we aren't going to militarize our schools with armed guards and combat-trained teachers — the offensive solution — are we ready for antiballistic armor in every classroom, perhaps in every kid's backpack — a defensive solution, but one that still makes schools seem like war zones?

The question says everything about how we handle broader societal fears: that defensive measures are the only solutions, not moderating our fears. We try to solve for every potential thing that could go wrong.

Supersized Fears

Plus, as it turns out, the odds of something going wrong are often overstated. A *LiveScience* article entitled "The Odds of Dying" describes how our perceptions of risk factors change over time as we learn more. For example, the chances of an Earth-impacting asteroid killing you was estimated in 1994 at about 1-in-20,000. Today, it's calculated as 1-in-500,000.

It's not that space rocks are jetting out of our solar system or being obliterated by NASA. Rather, the dramatic drop comes from a simple concept — we now know better. "A significant part of it is that we have now discovered, in the last dozen years, a good fraction of the largest, most deadly asteroids and found that they won't hit the Earth," a researcher says in the article.

Of course, sensationalized, creative causes of an untimely demise make great headlines. But they're also wildly overstated. Plane crashes seem common. But, as MIT researcher Arnold Barnett is quoted in the article, "You would need to fly every day for 123,000 years before being in a fatal crash."

Take a look at the table below with our odds of dying in various ways. Keep in mind that the odds of dying are 1-in-1; these are just the odds of particular possibilities.

We often fear acts of terrorism or airplane crashes — things we have nearly no control over — yet the most likely cause of death is heart disease — which we have quite a good amount of control over. Why?

A few key factors can fuel our misperceptions. At the Decision Research Institute in Oregon, Paul Slovic has spent his career studying how people judge risk. His research, as

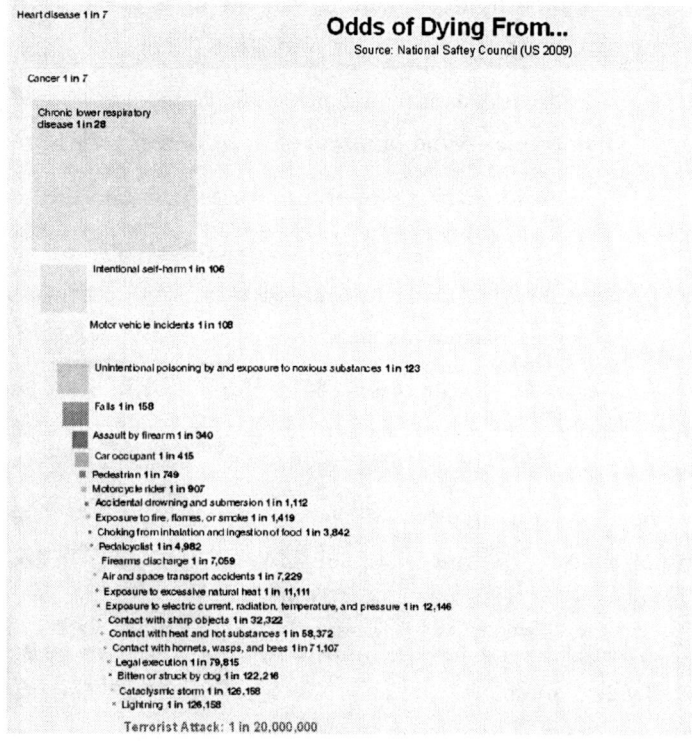

Odds of Dying From...
Source: National Saftey Council (US 2009)

Heart disease 1 in 7

Cancer 1 in 7

Chronic lower respiratory disease 1 in 28

Intentional self-harm 1 in 106

Motor vehicle incidents 1 in 108

Unintentional poisoning by and exposure to noxious substances 1 in 123

Falls 1 in 158

Assault by firearm 1 in 340

Car occupant 1 in 415

Pedestrian 1 in 749

Motorcycle rider 1 in 907

Accidental drowning and submersion 1 in 1,112

Exposure to fire, flames, or smoke 1 in 1,419

Choking from inhalation and ingestion of food 1 in 3,842

Pedalcyclist 1 in 4,982

Firearms discharge 1 in 7,059

Air and space transport accidents 1 in 7,229

Exposure to excessive natural heat 1 in 11,111

Exposure to electric current, radiation, temperature, and pressure 1 in 12,146

Contact with sharp objects 1 in 32,322

Contact with heat and hot substances 1 in 58,372

Contact with hornets, wasps, and bees 1 in 71,107

Legal execution 1 in 79,815

Bitten or struck by dog 1 in 122,216

Cataclysmic storm 1 in 126,158

Lightning 1 in 126,158

Terrorist Attack: 1 in 20,000,000

reported in an article on The Motley Fool, shows that people overestimate risk when a danger has a handful of qualities, including:

1. Catastrophic potential: Lots of people affected at once, rather than in small numbers over time.

2. Familiarity: A risk that isn't common knowledge.

3. Understanding: Something that doesn't seem understood by experts.

4. Personal control: A sense that danger is outside your control.

5. Voluntariness: Something can do harm even when you don't voluntarily put yourself in danger.

6. Children: A danger that affects the younger and more vulnerable — and innocent — members of society.

7. Victim identity: Level of familiarity with those who have suffered it.

8. Origin: Man-made risks are viewed as more dangerous than natural disasters.

A brief aside: similar biases contribute to fear in business organizations. The second section of this book will examine those factors.

Based on this list, it's easy to see why terrorist acts and school shootings create irrational levels of fear. And there's even more at hand in our always-on society.

A never-ceasing flow of information only amplifies these fear-feeding messages. Showing how technology can amplify fear responses, a recent study examined how Facebook can spread moods across the country. According to the study, rainy days in New York City affected the entire nation:

> Rain increased the number of negative Facebook posts by 1.16%, and decreased the number of positive posts by 1.19%. That observation set the stage for a natural experiment: How far would emotions motivated by rain spread through the social network? If New York City's rain-induced pathos could affect users in New Mexico, it would say something remarkable about the power of online emotional contagion.

And that's precisely what the researchers found. "If it rains in New York, people around the country become miserable," says study co-author Nicholas Christakis, professor of sociology and medicine at Yale University.

According to the chart of results, it wasn't only a New York City phenomenon — the Big Apple just happened to reverberate the most — the same effect happened in all major cities across the US.

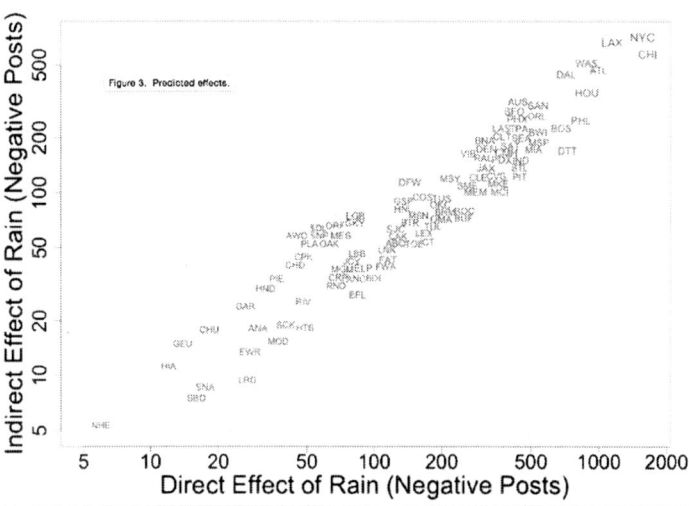

Figure 3. Predicted effects.

Perhaps the most egregious and ever present ways that our environment traps us in an echo chamber of fear is the marketing industry's attempts to get consumers to purchase their products.

Advertising messages are everywhere. Regardless of where we turn, we are inundated every second about the next must-have.

In 2007, the market research firm Yankelovich estimated that a person living in a city 30 years ago saw up to 2,000 ad messages a day, compared with up to 5,000 in 2007. And this was before the proliferation of social media and its embedded marketing messages amidst updates from friends and family — where we spend increasingly larger amounts of time.

More important than the amount of impressions is the nature of their messages. What are they reinforcing about our culture, relationships and safety? Mat Honan wrote an article in *Wired* magazine entitled "I Liked Everything I Saw on Facebook for Two Days. Here's What It Did to Me." The article describes the fear his experience created:

> My News Feed took on an entirely new character in a surprisingly short amount of time. After checking in and liking a bunch of stuff over the course of an hour, there were no human beings in my feed anymore. It became about brands and messaging, rather than humans with messages.
>
> As day one rolled into day two, I began dreading going to Facebook. It had become a temple of provocation. Just as my News Feed had drifted further and further right, so too did it drift further and further left. Rachel Maddow, *Raw Story, Mother Jones, Daily Kos,* and all sort of other leftie stuff was interspersed with items that are so far to the right I'm nearly afraid to like them for fear of ending up on some sort of watch list.
>
> This is a problem much bigger than Facebook. It reminded me of what can go wrong in society, and

why we now often talk at each other instead of to each other. We set up our political and social filter bubbles and they reinforce themselves — the things we read and watch have become hyper-niche and cater to our specific interests. We go down rabbit holes of special interests until we're lost in the queen's garden, cursing everyone above ground.

Add to this problem an ever-more-troubling trend of businesses communicating fear and reinforcing all the other messages of fear that already exist in our society — even from sparkler-phobic leadership — and you get a toxic, paranoia-inducing stew of messages shaping our attitudes and behaviors to be more afraid.

A *Fast Company* article, examining Mitsubishi's approach for its 2014 Mitsubishi Outlander, describes just how that can play out:

> You know who's concerned about safety? New parents. In the months leading up to a brand new human baby's arrival there are coffee table corners being padded, breakables being moved to higher shelf locations, household cleaning products and other poisonous liquids put under lock and key (or at least an elastic band around the cupboard handle).

> Are some new parenting tactics born out of paranoia over actual danger? Of course. But car safety isn't one of them.

> Mitsubishi and agency 180LA have launched a new campaign that uses that stellar safety record to pitch it as the perfect ride for new humans and their parents.

> Dubbed "#FirstRide," the campaign includes a series

of web shorts about three New York City families who all faced their own unique challenges leading up to the first day of their child's life, and gives them a ride home from the hospital.

Perhaps it is a chicken/egg discussion in terms of which comes first. Is it the marketing that creates the anxiety and fear, or is it our society that creates the fear for marketing to tap into? Either way, it's a self-feeding cycle.

Personally, I have become so offended by corporate attempts to tap into America's worst fears that I seek to do business only with companies who tap into hopes and dreams. I've found that these companies also tell me more: they have to show how their features provide some utility that can unlock something new in my life, not merely guard against some concern. Compared to helping me discover new value, marketing fear just seems lazy.

A 2012 article in *The Conference Board Review* notes the success of marketing fear:

> The sunscreen industry was founded on a real fear. But its multi-product expansion, to everything from facial wash to shampoos, is marketed on the same trepidations, because whether it is real or exaggerated, fear sells. It always has. Fear is what moves insurance policies, weight-loss systems, and Rogaine. It is why women will spend more for an anti-wrinkle cream if it has microbeads and why Viagra sales are almost $2 billion globally. Fear convinces people to invest in GPS systems for their cars and cell phones for their teenagers.

The marketing message behind all of these products is the same: If you don't buy it, something bad will happen. You'll get fat. You'll go bald. You won't perform. No one will love you. Your family will be left homeless and penniless. You'll be an outcast.

Entire industries thrive on fear.

For those in the advertising and marketing industries, fear is a standard approach to pushing product. While there are some voices discussing the ethical dilemma of using the approach, most are motivated, ironically enough, by fear of consumer backlash. As the article concludes, "The challenge is in packaging the message of fear while still leaving the customer with a positive connection toward your brand."

Doesn't seem to be a problem if $300 backpack sales are skyrocketing.

Money Conjures Fears

Fear isn't limited to the extraordinary. We also see fear in the mundane — and this, too, is growing in American society. While there are no reliable studies on what subjects dominate our thoughts, it is a safe bet that money ranks at or near the top — and money fears are at or near the top of most Americans' concerns.

A proxy for such a study is how we spend our time. The US Bureau of Labor Statistics released a study on our time in 2013, and the *International Business Times* put together the following infographics to show the activities we spend time on and how they've changed since 2003.

Daily	Minutes	% Change in 10 Years
Sleeping	490	0.4%
Working	359	3.8%
TV & Movies	131	8.3%
Eating & Drinking	131	3.1%
Washing, Dressing & Grooming	67	2.4%
Socializing & Time w/ Others	31	-6.1%
Commuting to Work	31	6.9%
Caring for Children	20	0.0%
Cooking	19	5.6%
Relaxing or Thinking	13	-18.8%
Cleaning & Home Upkeep	16	6.7%

Weekly

	Minutes	% Change in 10 Years
Shopping	228	-5.6%
Sports, Exercise & Recreation	112	0.0%
Reading for Pleasure	91	-7.1%
Travel for Socializing	70	0.0%
Computer Use - Leisure	63	28.6%
Laundry	56	-11.1%
Lawn / Garden	56	-27.3%
Travel for Eating / Drinking	56	14.3%
Religious Practices or Services	49	0.0%
Playing Games	42	0.0%

Monthly

	Minutes	% Change in 10 Years
Caring & Helping Non-household members	180	-25.0%
Volunteer Activities	180	0.0%
Attending Parties / Events	120	-20.0%

The trend that emerges when you study these charts is that we spend more of our time on selfish pursuits. Less time on activities with and for others; more time doing things that are personally enjoyable or earning money to fund those things. Less time caring for others, being in social settings, and relaxing; more time with media, entertainment, travel, and leisure.

As we spend more time earning, spending, and subsequently thinking about money, we show that our attitudes related to money are rooted in fear. Fear of not having enough, uncertainty about future earnings, or fear of losing what we do have. Coming out of the Great Recession has obviously shaped those attitudes, but they are not the only influences on our money-related fearfulness.

A 2013 CNBC article comments on Americans' attitudes toward investing five years after the Great Recession:

> Five years after US investment bank Lehman Brothers collapsed, triggering a global financial crisis and shattering confidence worldwide, families in major countries around the world are still hunkered down, too spooked and distrustful to take chances with their money.
>
> An Associated Press analysis of households in the 10 biggest economies shows that families continue to spend cautiously and have pulled hundreds of billions of dollars out of stocks, cut borrowing for the first time in decades and poured money into savings and bonds that offer puny interest payments, often too low to keep up with inflation.
>
> "It doesn't take very much to destroy confidence, but

it takes an awful lot to build it back," says Ian Bright, senior economist at ING, a global bank based in Amsterdam. "The attitude toward risk is permanently reset." A flight to safety on such a global scale is unprecedented since the end of World War II.

Fear has gripped our personal financial decisions so strongly that we would rather earn less of a return on our money than inflation. We apparently would rather destroy wealth knowingly rather than take a risk with equity markets.

A *Time* magazine article about the economy in the summer of 2013 uses Las Vegas as an example of the new economic reality facing the US after the Great Recession:

> Las Vegas' situation might now be raising a broader economic issue. If we can't let loose with money there, does it mean that a nation raised on risk — from gold-seeking Forty-Niners to Texas wildcatters to Wall Street arbitrageurs — has lost its appetite? Banks have been criticized for refusing to let go of the money. Corporations have trillions of dollars sitting on balance sheets because they're wary of taking on too big an investment risk.
>
> Mutual-fund investors pulled billions of dollars out of equities for four years running until early this year, missing a huge jackpot as the market reached record levels. Stocks compensate for risk better than roulette tables do, so if scarred consumers are unwilling to invest in Wall Street, it's not necessarily surprising that when they come to Vegas, they are betting less, playing different games — or not playing at all.

But fears aren't limited to saving, investing, and spending money. The massive accumulation of debt is also creating fears. Debt creates more financial fear by being an immediate obligation that can have dire financial consequences for decades. A 2013 Literacy Survey conducted by The National Foundation for Credit Counseling indicates that 77% of American adults have "financial worries" and cite "not having enough savings, losing my job, and not being able to pay certain financial obligations" as drivers for their worries.

To underscore how big this problem has become, look no further than the 20-year history of debt accumulation in the run-up to the Great Recession as demonstrated by this chart from the Federal Reserve.

Household Debt and Disposable Income
Billions of dollars; quarterly

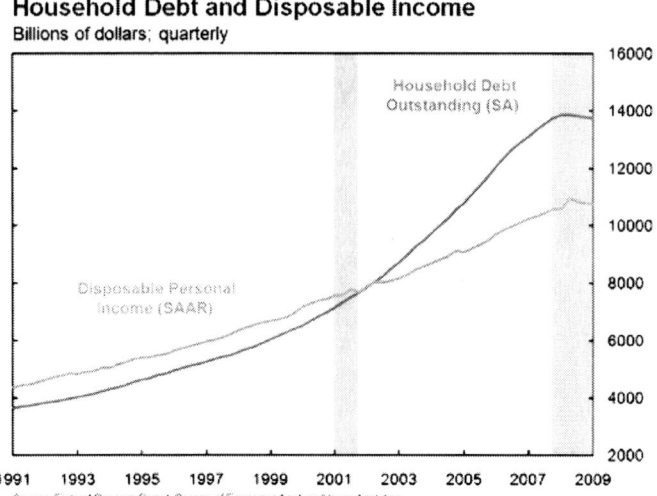

While this trend has recently reversed due to households getting their finances in order, it is obvious how it could have colored our attitudes toward money with fear.

In short, fear is everywhere.

A little less short, fear today is thriving in our leadership trying to guard against every possible danger, in our irrational perceptions of what could cause us harm, in the constant stream of fear-based messages in media and marketing, and even in our most basic and practical financial situations.

3
FEAR IS RUINING CORPORATE AMERICA

"The major problem we deal with is that fear is the most prominent factor in people's decision-making process. And you can actually measure it as several multiples greater than euphoria or greed."

— Alan Greenspan

FORMER FEDERAL RESERVE Chair Alan Greenspan made those comments in 2013. Considering that he coined the term "irrational exuberance" during the run-up to the Internet stock bubble, his words should carry a real warning about the psyche of American business and the danger of fear.

Risk-taking made America great. We weren't afraid, so we out-maneuvered the rest of the world. We set audacious goals and risked our life savings. And we thrived.

It's even in our genes. In 2013, *Time* magazine ran a cover article on happiness, including a discussion about biological differences related to risk-taking:

> Investigators at Harvard and Boston University analyzed a gene, 5-HTTLPR, related to serotonin transport. The allele of that gene that codes for anxiety and risk avoidance is less common in individualistic cultures like that of the US.

Not only are we genetically pre-disposed to be risk-takers, our history is marked by opportunity-seekers, dating back to Ellis Island and our great-great-grandparents' desire to take part in a growing America.

The historical context of our immigrant forefathers makes our current level of fear — as seen in a recent *USA Today* headline: "Is too little market fear something to fear?" — that much more surprising.

Even immigration scares us. The very thing that allowed our forefathers to come to America and thrive is now something that divides us and causes us to worry about our future.

To drive the point home, the article quotes an annual happiness study in which the US ranked 23rd out of 50 countries — far behind first-ranked Iceland, and also trailing Singapore, Malaysia, Tanzania, and Vietnam. I am not trying to suggest that fear equals lack of happiness, but our nation's culture, through fear or otherwise, isn't just causing us to avoid risk. It's robbing us of our joy.

Is America Still an Entrepreneurial Leader?

A 2008 study by the Brookings Institute showed that business destruction was outpacing business creation — perhaps for the first time in the nation's history. It isn't that companies are failing more, but rather that there is a drought of new business creation. A big reason for this trend is fear of failure.

The U.S. economy has become less entrepreneurial over time
Share of new and dissolving firms, 1978–2011

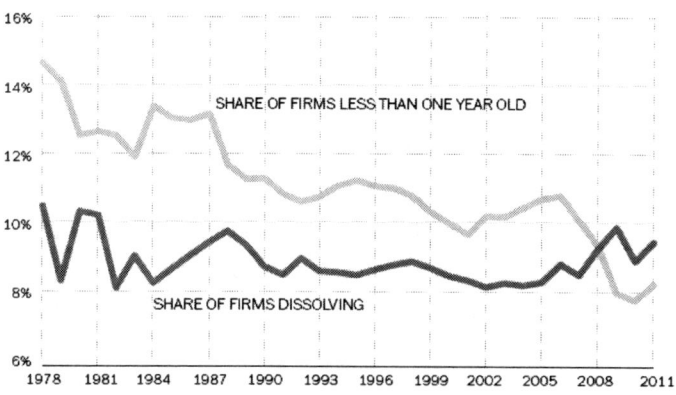

SOURCE: Brookings Institution calculations from U.S. Census Bureau data
GRAPHIC: The Washington Post. Published May 5, 2014

When starting a child-care business in 2004, I had that exact fear. My wife and I were a young couple. We had only been married a year. We were trying to establish ourselves financially. When we built the concept of BabysitEase, funding felt like a major impediment — not just the start-up costs but also our foregone earnings.

We had limited cash savings outside of our retirement accounts, and our monthly budget would have gone into a deficit if we had taken away my wife's income. We thought we were brave enough to tackle one of the two funding problems, but tackling both seemed daunting. As we planned her exit from a corporate job, we had to make some sacrifices. Selling a car and cutting back helped, but start-up capital was still a bit of a challenge. We weren't sure what to do.

I entered our business plan into a competition at the University of Cincinnati, where I was a graduate student, and won $2,500 through a bridge fund. We sunk that money — and eventually more — into a website that provided the platform for our business processes. And we launched.

$2,500. That was all it took. Looking back, I can't believe that $2,500 might have held us back from business success, family freedom, and flexibility. We had $2,500, but a psychological barrier prevented us from risking our own money to get the business off the ground. It took winning the money to make us feel committed. The fear of loss is a real impediment to economic success when our culture doesn't promote the risk-taking that is needed to be successful.

My experience isn't unique. Fewer people are taking economic risks. Roughly 3.6% of households headed by adults younger than 30 own stakes in private companies, compared with 10.6% in 1989 — when the central bank began collecting standard data on Americans' incomes and net worth — and 6.1% in 2010. The number of young adults who start a business dropped in 2013 to its lowest level in at least 17 years. Overall, the US startup rate — new firms as a portion of all firms — fell by nearly half between 1978 and 2011.

According to a *Wall Street Journal* article entitled "Endangered Species: Young US Entrepreneurs," the decline in business ownership among young graduates also reflects a relatively low appetite for risk:

> "Young people have less confidence," said Donna Kelley, a professor at Babson College. In an annual survey she oversees, more than 41% of 25–34-year-old Americans who saw an opportunity to start a business said fear of failure would keep them from doing so, up from 23.9% in 2001. "The fear of failure is the measure we should be most concerned about," she said.

Fear's impact on our competitiveness is clear. The 2012 Global Entrepreneurship Monitor's report describes the environment for new business creation around the world:

> Risk-taking can pose considerable challenges for potential entrepreneurs. Universities and business schools around the world can generally teach the basics of entrepreneurship, boosting peoples' abilities to perceive opportunities and their skills for starting businesses. A key stumbling block, however, is one's inherent fear of failure. This can counteract the drive to start a business, even when the expected returns from entrepreneurship have better prospects than the next best alternative. People may have differing levels of fear of failure and conditions in the institutional environment, such as bankruptcy legislation, which could deter would-be entrepreneurs.

As the name suggests, this is a global report, and skeptics could argue that its results are skewed by participants lacking the opportunities present in the US. But the GEM also compared countries, and these results show that the US is lagging:

> The level of fear of failure, in general, increases as one moves from early-stage to advanced development levels. Greece (61%) and Italy (58%) exhibited the highest fear of failure rates in 2012, consistent with the low reported opportunity perceptions in these economies. Malawi (12%), a factor-driven economy, showed the lowest fear of failure rate.

Across the geographic regions, fear of failure rates show less distinction than do opportunity and capability perceptions. Economies in Sub-Saharan Africa tend to show the lowest levels, with only 25% of all respondents indicating that fear of failure would prevent them from starting a business. Latin American and Caribbean economies (28%) also have low levels of this measure.

In short, countries with the most to lose in terms of real economic value — like the opportunity cost of leaving a high-paying job, blowing through a savings or retirement account, etc. — were the countries showing the most fear. And most Americans have plenty to lose. Fear is very much a part of the US business culture.

Owning Fear

This brings up an important point in fear dynamics: the role of ownership. The concept of ownership is an important one in the American story. Land ownership has long been an iconic tale — consider the scene in the movie *Far & Away* where

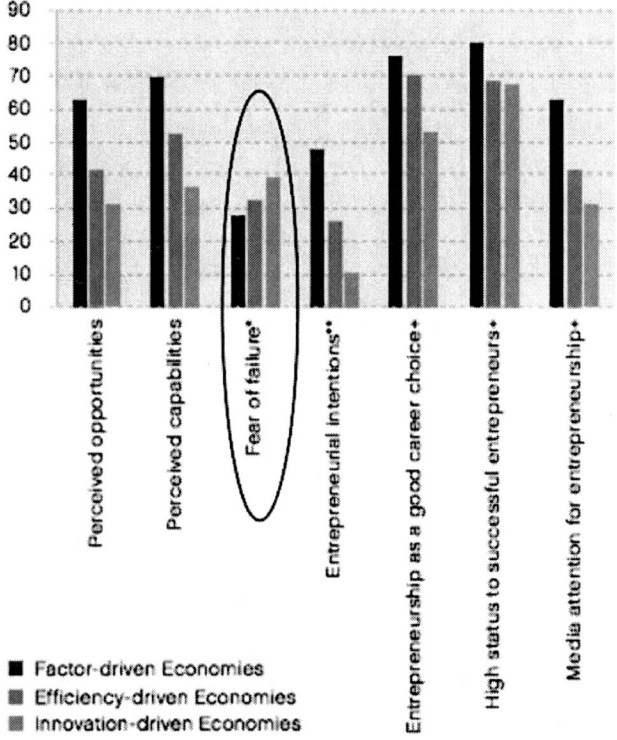

- Factor-driven Economies
- Efficiency-driven Economies
- Innovation-driven Economies

* Fear of failure assessed for those seeing opportunities

** Intentions assessed among nonentrepreneur population

\+ These questions were optional and therefore not included by all economies

Tom Cruise rushes across the Kansas countryside, racing thousands of others on horseback to plant his flag on the plot of land that would become their family's heritage.

But beyond land, the concept of ownership is a powerful motivator and an important part of what made America's economic system such a dominant one for the past 200 years. The downside of ownership, however, is that having something of value makes it easy to focus on not losing it rather than on growing it and making it work for you. An owned asset can be seen as fallback — the thing that can help bail you out when times get tough. It can become a corrupting agent much like what the ring does to Gollum in the *Lord of the Rings* trilogy.

This concept plays out in one of Jesus's parables:

> For it will be like a man going on a journey, who called his servants and entrusted to them his property. To one he gave five talents, to another two, to another one, to each according to his ability. Then he went away. He who had received the five talents went at once and traded with them, and he made five talents more. So also he who had the two talents made two talents more. But he who had received the one talent went and dug in the ground and hid his master's money. Now after a long time the master of those servants came and settled accounts with them. And he who had received the five talents came forward, bringing five talents more, saying, "Master, you delivered to me five talents; here I have made five talents more." His master said to him, "Well done, good and faithful servant." He also who had received the one talent came forward, saying, "Master, I knew you to be a hard man, reaping where you did not sow, and gathering where you scattered no seed, so I was afraid, and I went and hid your talent in the ground. Here you have what is yours." But his master answered him, "You wicked and slothful servant! You

knew that I reap where I have not sown and gather where I scattered no seed? Then you ought to have invested my money with the bankers, and at my coming I should have received what was my own with interest.

Notice that the underlying motivation behind the desire to hide the asset was fear.

Ask any parent with a small child what happens when they get a new toy — and if the parent tries to take it back. "Mine! Mine!" As parents we spend a vast amount of time trying to reprogram the idea of ownership by teaching the basic principle of sharing.

This same basic premise occurs in our business lives. The statistics and stories above show how it plays out in entrepreneurship and individual decisions, and corporations develop this same aversion to risking something they have for the promise of the next great business possibility.

The Public Company Pressure

While we will address the individual factors that influence the amount of fear in a corporate culture in the next several chapters, one important factor on a global basis is the nature of financial markets and their impact on public companies.

The tension of short-term versus long-term goals of a business has never come into more stark contrast than in the past few decades. Advances in technology have led investors to take an increasingly shorter-term view on profits, increasing the pressure that corporations feel.

Marc Andreesen — who founded Netscape, the first consumer web browser and responsible for the explosion of the internet that we know today — had this to say about being a public company CEO after the dawn of the 21st century:

> You've had a dramatic rise in hedge funds. Very short-term trading and dramatic rise in short-selling [investors betting that a stock's price will fall]. If you're a public company, you become the shuttlecock between warring longs and shorts. They bat your stock around like it's a chew toy.

It's a quarter-to-quarter treadmill. Active shareholders see opportunities to get in and get out after forcing the sale of an ancillary business. Increasing amounts of executive pay are tied to stock performance. It's all led to an overall mindset that lacks patience, vision, and courage. In its place is a general mentality of faster-and-bigger profits, get-results-now, do-whatever-it-takes.

This phenomenon is exacerbated in the stock market. Investors strive to create new technology that focus on profits not from quarter-to-quarter or month-to-month, but from milliseconds between trades.

Take a look at the exhibit below from the *New York Times* to illustrate the impact of high-frequency-trading activity. The line at the bottom of this graphic is the stock-market activity involving General Electric (GE) shares over 100 milliseconds at 12:44 p.m. on Dec. 19, 2013. The gray box magnifies a five-millisecond window, during which GE experienced heavy bid-and-offer activity and a total of 44 trades.

For context, the article gives examples of things that occur within one millisecond.

1 Millisecond	100 Milliseconds	200 Milliseconds	1 Second
500 Quote changes & 150 stock trades	1 Fast blink of the human eye	Time it takes your brain to recognize a word after your eyes see it.	Single heartbeat of an adult at rest
Single pixel on a high-end TV changes colors	Venus flytrap snaps shut		Cruising speed of Boeing 747 travels 832 feet.

This financial model has large repercussions on founders, CEOs, and other corporate executives. It shapes how they lead their organizations, often to the detriment of what would be most effective in the long-term. It has even begun to turn businesses away from going public.

In a recent KPMG survey of 91 US startups, 45% of

respondents said they prefer to remain private, more than 30% want to be acquired, and only 19% want to go public. This desire to avoid all the negative impacts of being a public company has led to a dramatic decline in the number of companies choosing to go public over the past decade as shown in this figure.

The U.S. IPO market collapsed

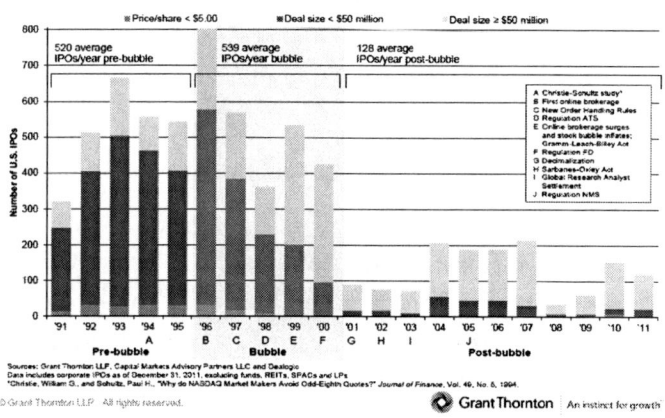

Forbes magazine does an annual feature on private companies. In the 2013 edition of that feature — entitled "The Six Habits of Successful Private Companies" — Bruce Upbin writes:

> It's a good time again to be a privately held company. No pressure over quarterly earnings, no obsession with stock prices, no anxiety over what you can say to whom about how the business is going. Heck, nobody outside the owner has to know anything.

The pressures Upbin points out are largely focused on the

most senior managers or those involved in the financial reporting process, and they lead to a larger, more dangerous mindsets in publicly traded companies.

With a built-in fear factor from the constant pressure for
short-term results, the incentive for loyalty vanishes. When
clouds appear on the horizon, sticking it out is not an appealing option. It only presents a downside: reduced pay. On
the other hand, moving to a different company presents a
nice upside: a chance to ensure a more certain income. And,
beyond striving to satisfy ever-increasing earnings expectations, managers often over-reach in order to feed the value of
their own stock options.

Needless to say, short-term mentalities are not healthy for
long-term business growth.

A recent example is Sam Palmisano, the former CEO of
IBM. At an investor conference on May 12, 2010, he pledged
that per-share earnings would reach $20 in five years, a plan
called Roadmap 2015. The context for this pledge: IBM's
stock had stagnated. For the six months prior, the stock had
dropped 1.5% while the Dow had risen 3%. There was some
pressure to put a little spark back in the stock. Palmisano's
pledge achieved exactly that. The stock slightly outperformed
the broader market over the next six months.

However, the pledge's long-term impact was company-
threatening. In May 2014, *Bloomberg Business* ran a cover story
on the situation entitled "The Trouble with IBM," chronicling
how the pledge had handcuffed then-CEO Ginni Rometty.
Rometty could have shown long-term leadership by cancel-
ling the plan and readying the company to take advantage of
the shifting technology landscape. But she likely would have

been punished with a short-term stock drop. So, even though it would normalized over time and positioned IBM to excel over the next five years instead of just the next five quarters, she couldn't.

The story describes the fallout:

> In interviews, and even in public Internet posts, employees refer to the plan bitterly as Roadkill 2015. To make earnings rise while revenue is falling, Rometty has cut costs, sold business lines, fired workers, figured out ways to lower IBM's tax rate, bought back shares, and taken on debt. Of the 25 analysts tracked by Bloomberg, nine predict that IBM will indeed hit the $20 target. The question is what type of company Rometty will have left when she gets there.

All from the fear of short-term investor pressure.

While this pressure only impacts organizations that are publicly traded, it's analogous to the fears that nearly all businesses face. Which is exactly what this book is about. We will explore eight common fear factors over the next several chapters. They fall into three categories: cultural core, external factors, and advisory services.

The cultural core. Management and decision-making, individuality, and politics are the key aspects of any organization. They are its central nervous system. Fear, like Parkinson's Disease, kills off healthy aspects and affects the organization's ability to create value through healthy decision-making.

External factors. Outside events and circumstances have the ability to knock any organization off-course without warning, sometimes leaving the organization feeling like it has no control over the outcome. These factors include competition, media, and regulation. While it is good to be aware of these factors and even put systems in place to keep them from bringing harm to the organization, they should not be feared. Rather, they should be approached with a healthy understanding of their real impact and preparation for how to respond when they come knocking. We'll focus on how to avoid having the fear of these things push an organization to become something that it is not.

Advisory services. Lastly, there are advisory services, internal and external, that can wreak havoc. We'll focus primarily on legal and risk management advisors, but it could be management consultants or other advisors with agendas beyond an organization's needs. It is important to understand the role of advisors and check their power and influence before the fear they can breed causes missed opportunities.

Control and Fear: A Cycle

At the heart of each of these factors is the need for control. As Americans, we've been programmed to get things and accumulate them — whether money, friends, food, hobbies, or sexual conquests. Once we have the thing we seek, we have something to lose. Thus, the fear cycle begins.

With something to lose — a career, great salary, market leadership — the sense of ownership creates fear. Our natural response is to reach for control. Control over people, control through technology or control through processes. These controls reinforce our sense of ownership, causing the fear cycle to grow all the more.

However, this reach for certainty and stability provide no guarantees of safety. Often, they do just the opposite, generating other negative consequences worse than the very thing they were trying to control. As you read each of the next eight chapters, consider how the fear cycle could be affecting — and infecting — your business.

THE FEAR CYCLE

4

FEAR INDICATOR 1 – MANAGEMENT & DECISION-MAKING

"While high trust won't necessarily rescue a poor strategy, low trust will almost always derail a good one."

— Stephen Covey

FOR THE PAST 40 years — years of Vietnam, Watergate, junk bonds, Monica Lewinsky, Enron, the Catholic Church sex scandals, the Iraq war — our trust in each other has been dropping steadily. Trust in many institutions, too, has been seriously shaken. The General Social Survey, a periodic assessment of Americans' moods and values, shows a 10-point decline from 1976 to 2006 in the number of Americans who believe other people can generally be trusted. The General Social Survey also shows declines in trust in our institutions, sometimes linked to specific events like the ones above. From the 1970s to today, trust has declined in the press (24% to 11%), education (36% to 28%), banks (35% to 31%), corporations (26% to 17%), and organized religion (35% to 25%).

While most of the General Social Survey's points are associated with institutional trust, there is a broader aspect of mistrust affecting our individual relationships and showing up in the institutional mistrust reflected in those survey results. As Jeremy Adam Smith, a fellow at the Institute for Justice and Journalism, notes, "Trust no one" has essentially served as Americans' motto over the last two generations. To dig further into the individual relationship aspect of mistrust, Smith says:

> For starters, trust in others depends on how much contact people have with other people — and Americans today are measurably more isolated than previous generations. They have fewer close friends, for example, and are less likely to join voluntary associations such as bird-watching groups and church choirs. This is important, because people who belong to such associations tend to become more trusting as a consequence. Experiments, as well as experience, show that people trust people they know before they trust strangers — and so the more people you know, the more you trust.

Mistrust, a common root of fear, kills relationships. A spouse who is convinced their partner is having an affair can create the very mistrust that they are so afraid of. This fear, causing paranoid behavior like constantly checking the other's cell phone for texts or pictures, can kill the very intimacy it's hoping to protect. The same thing happens in business, creating a culture of fear that is hard to overcome on the path toward business results.

If you believe business success depends on people working together for a common goal, mistrust has serious implications on manager promotions, hiring practices, team norming, and building trust within and across teams. All things that are afterthoughts in most organizations and get only scraps of energy and time on a day-to-day basis.

If mistrust permeates a business, it creates a fear that clouds our judgment and pushes us in directions that are off our business plan. This fear manifests itself in many ways, and we'll outline a few particularly egregious examples along with how they can create disastrous effects on an organization's ability to execute effectively.

Mistrust in Executive Pay

Nowhere is the growing sentiment of mistrust more evident than in executive pay packages.

According to the Economic Policy Institute, CEOs are getting raises far bigger and faster than the people they employ. On average, executive pay is nearly 273 times that of a production employee.

Perhaps more dramatic than the ratio itself is how the gap has widened over the past half-century. In 1965, an average CEO took home slightly more than 20 times what an average production/non-supervisory employee earned. That ratio moved upward slowly throughout the decades of the 60s,

70s, and 80s, then soared in the 90s. Even with dips in the ratio in 2002 and 2009, it has stayed far above that of previous decades.

Bloomberg Business ran an article in 2013 about the growing size of "golden parachutes" — the severance plans of publicly traded company CEOs. The article includes a graphic demonstrating the relative size of the top ten severance plans, ranging in size from $104.8 million for Robert Iger of Disney to $303.4 million for John Hammergren at McKesson. The article notes the problem these golden parachutes create:

> "If you have a safety net of this type of gargantuan
> size, it starts to undermine the CEO's desire to build
> long-term value for shareholders," says Paul Hodgson,
> a director at corporate governance researcher BHJ
> Partners. "You don't really care if you're fired or not."

Such an attitude is a big problem for CEOs who are trying to rally their workforces towards a common business plan, strategy, or vision for the future — which requires that they buy in to a long-term perspective. It not only drives a wedge of mistrust and fear between executives and staff, but also creates subliminal fear in the executives themselves. When focused on protecting what they have or what they can continue to accumulate, executives are far less likely to make good, bold decisions that create lasting, long-term value for the organization.

Mickey Drexler, the former CEO of Gap and current CEO of J. Crew, said this about these growing behaviors in the executive suite:

> America's companies are built to destroy creativity. If
> you become the head of a big company today, you're

not the youngest person in the world. You have a contract. You get a jet. You have a huge overpaid salary. You get bonuses. Do you think that CEO is going to screw around with fast, creative change? No. And the Board of Directors, the last thing they want is someone who's going to change things.

And it isn't just direct pay and compensation that erodes trust. In a *Harvard Business Review* article, William Lazonick, professor of economics at the University of Massachusetts-Lowell, talks about how CEOs are also using corporate capital to enrich the value of this direct compensation — at the expense of their company's long-term futures. He cites the following data points as evidence of the me-first attitude behind the short-term focus that has led to mistrust of management:

Between 2003 and 2012, publicly listed firms in the S&P 500 used a colossal amount of their earnings — 54% or $2.4 trillion — to buy back their own stock.

Net disinvestment: "the amount of stock taken out of the market has exceeded the amount issued in almost every year; from 2004 through 2013, this net withdrawal averaged $316 billion a year."

With 54% of earnings going to share buybacks, and 37% going out in dividends, there is little left for investing in innovation.

When employees see this sort of activity — not long-term decision-making — it's no wonder they lose trust in the golden-parachuted, lavishly paid executives.

Mistrust in Management

While executive pay and compensation may have a significant impact on a culture of fear, it can seem too academic, unapproachable for the average businessperson. We become numb to the numbers. But management quality is something we all have personal experience with — and has broader implications than executive pay.

I want to start by saying that I have been blessed with truly outstanding managers in my time in corporate America. Disproportionately so, based on my conversations with friends and peers.

In my first job at Arthur Andersen, I worked for a senior manager named Dan Fagin. He was not overly inspirational or highly skilled technically, but what he lacked in those areas, he made up for in spades with his interest and genuine care for his employees.

I happened to work at Arthur Andersen during the Enron implosion. As you may know, Andersen was the audit firm that represented Enron and got pulled into the public backlash. There were SEC investigations and client defections. Each day led to a new *Wall Street Journal* article about what role the firm had in helping Enron senior managers perpetrate one of the largest corporate frauds in American history.

As you could imagine, it was a very difficult period to be a member of the firm. We had regular town hall meetings in the mornings. The Office Managing Partner "rallied the troops" and "reassured everyone" that the firm would escape the negative press as long as we avoided panicky decisions.

Walking back to our cubes, we always felt stunned at the

apparent disconnect our senior managers had. Then, Dan would pull us into his office and shoot straight with us. I remember one particular exchange where he said, "I would tell you if the wheels were falling off the bus. We do have a few flat tires."

We all appreciated the candor alone. But, beyond being honest, he followed the discussion with his own plans. He let us know that he was talking with firms in the area and that there were several options for us. We just needed to sit tight. When there was a decision to make, he told us, we would sit down and make it as a team.

And that is exactly what we did. Several weeks later, we had dinner together, and he presented three options. We weighed the pros and cons together as a team, and he supported our decision, possibly even at the cost of his own personal financial gain. He did so because he understood the power of a close team, and he knew the trust that he built through this process would propel us all to greater success.

But for every Dan Fagin, there is an anti-Dan Fagin. While good managers create trust, confidence, and good decision-making environments, horrible manager experiences create a cultural fear that washes over teams and organizations, pushing high performers out the door faster than any other cause.

At an insurance company, I had the good fortune of working for two amazing executives who were supportive, gave me stretch opportunities, and allowed me to fail while supporting me as I learned. However, in my last year there, my boss retired. The man who took over was a good man, but he struggled to take a position and avoided hard conversations.

Under him, one of my first initiatives was to find a second

processing facility on the West Coast. I felt this second location was critical to our growth, providing capabilities and continuity opportunities that would allow us to sell to the largest banks in the country.

While on a trip to scout a possible location, I received an email from a peer. For an important initiative of his own, he was looking for a few resources, requiring only the ability to work with Excel spreadsheets. While I had responsibility for a large number of resources, our team at the time was stretched thin. In a brief response, as I rushed between the airport gate and my rental car, I suggested he look at a temporary staffing firm that we used regularly and offered to help him procure the people as soon as I returned. I indicated that we could have him the resources through the staffing agency by early the following week.

After a busy day meeting with those responsible for the office locations and performing due diligence and negotiations on the facility, I checked my email. There was a message from my boss. He wrote that my email was being seen by the executive team as uncooperative — but not because of my suggestion in and of itself; rather, from my peer's one-sided characterization of it. My boss, without ever asking for my perspective of the situation, added that this lack of cooperation was going to affect me negatively in the future.

His email, which I read in my hotel room thousands of miles from the office, after a long day of travel, meetings, and negotiations, hit me like a bunker-busting bomb. Mistrust didn't creep in; it knocked down the door to my psyche and changed my decision-making mindset. At that moment, my manager lost me. Demoralized and frustrated by a succession of such examples, I left seven months later.

Sadly, we all have a personal example of this loss of trust, a life-long scar on our ability to act confidently. These moments are always present in the quiet of our thoughts like the devil on the shoulder in those old Bugs Bunny cartoons. They are the whispers of doubt that lead to fearful decisions and keep us from being brave in everything from small decisions to big, strategic, game changing ways.

Not only does management dysfunction make us fearful in a corporate context, but, said another way, it kills employee engagement. Gallup, the famous polling organization, does an annual study on the level of employee engagement in organizations across the world. Each year this report is scoured by HR, business management, and academics for insight into how our cultures and behaviors can improve organizational effectiveness. An excerpt from their most recent report begins with a warning:

> At Gallup, we've studied the impact of human nature on the economy for decades. We've now reviewed more than 25 million responses to our employee engagement survey, the Q12. And what we found out about managers and employees has serious implications for the future of American companies and the world.

The rest of the report is a depressing read with a litany of stats that all point to one primary cause: bad management behavior. It sows the contagion of fear one employee at a time, but does so broadly enough to make entire organizations ineffective. The Gallup report sums it up with this synopsis:

Of the approximately 100 million people in America who hold full-time jobs, 30 million (30%) are engaged and inspired at work, so we can assume they have a great boss. At the other end of the spectrum are roughly 20 million (20%) employees who are actively disengaged. These employees, who have bosses from hell that make them miserable, roam the halls spreading discontent. The other 50 million (50%) American workers are not engaged. They're just kind of present, but not inspired by their work or their managers.

Despite the efforts of new and innovative management practices, increased management training, and a slew of other approaches to increase engagement, the 30% engagement level quoted by Gallup hasn't budged in a decade. It ebbs and flows a bit year-to-year, but on the whole, it's remained flat.

So why hasn't the needle moved on engagement? Gallup believes it has to do with our hiring practices:

Whom companies name as manager is one of the most important decisions they make given that managers play a critical role in driving engagement in any organization. Whether hiring from the outside or promoting from within, organizations that scientifically select managers for the unique talents it takes to effectively manage people greatly increase the odds of employee engagement. Instead of using management jobs as promotional prizes for all career paths, companies should treat them as unique roles with distinct functional demands that require a specific talent set. The reality is that many people who are the best performers in their current roles do not have the talents necessary to effectively manage people.

Management and supervision is necessary. There must be a final decision-maker. There has to be someone who can stay focused on the vision for the company and keep the day-to-day actions true to that vision. Someone who can take an objective look at performance and make course corrections along the way. The right person creates trust. The wrong person creates fear. And, as statistics and stories both show, there aren't a lot of the right people currently out there.

Organizational Hierarchies

We know that managers can create — and more often than not are creating — fear. What about the overall structure in which they exist? What role does hierarchy itself have in creating a culture of fear?

In 2010, Cameron Anderson and Courtney Brown of the UC Berkeley Haas School of Business wrote a summary of popular research on hierarchy's effects on performance. After looking through many studies, their conclusive answer is: it depends. Sometimes hierarchy helps. Sometimes not.

When the work was complex, taller hierarchical structures hurt performance. They also led to breakdowns in communication, worsening results further. On the other hand, looser structures yielded faster solutions and fewer errors. With simpler tasks, though, clear central hierarchies improved performance and accelerated problem solving.

What didn't change, however, was how people felt about centralized hierarchies:

> While the results of many organizational studies have been mixed regarding the effects of steeper hierarchy on performance, studies have been highly consistent regarding the effects of steeper hierarchy on members' attitudes. Groups and organizations with steeper hierarchies tended to have members who were less satisfied, less motivated, and more inclined to leave the group.

> The effects of hierarchy steepness will depend on whether groups select the right individuals as leaders – for example, individuals who are collectively minded, unbiased in their decision-making, use a more democratic style of leadership, and who are technically expert.

While organizational structure may or may not have an impact on performance, it regularly affects individuals' mindsets. The descriptions that Anderson and Brown use — "less satisfied," "less motivated," "more inclined to leave" — sound an awful lot like the mindset of someone who has lost trust in their leadership. An awful lot like manager experiences we've all had and hated. And I'm not talking about the Dan Fagin experiences.

So how do we avoid mistrust in organizational structure? A few brave souls are trying a much more democratic organization built on the collective wisdom of peers. Matthew Prince of CloudFlare, a company that now processes 250 billion page views a month through its security apps, was interviewed for an article in *Inc. Magazine*. The article focuses on how CloudFlare has given up on titles altogether.

On the wisdom of not providing such a "cheap perk" for employees, Prince is quoted as saying, "Oh, no — titles definitely come with a cost. The best ideas are bottom-up, not top-down. But in most companies, the ideas come from the top, and hierarchy can mean artificial authority wins, not the best idea." The interviewer pushes the question further and asks about the impact on their customers. Prince continues:

> A major New York City bank asked us to send our most senior people to a meeting recently. We brought engineers — and all the decision-makers loved the fact the people in the room were the ones who actually write the code. People just want their problems solved, and titles don't solve problems — talented people solve problems.

I have experienced this first hand while running the administrative functions at my current company, Epipheo. We don't have a strong hierarchy at all. Rather, we use the collective wisdom of the entire organization to drive results.

How? Through functions like a weekly all-company meeting for reviewing our work. We screen each completed video and allow everyone in the company to rate each one. While it is often easy to see who the most talented people are in an organization, this collective wisdom puts empirical evidence behind pay and promotion decisions — usually affirming subjective intuition. This democratic metric adds both insight and confidence when determining organizational power for future jobs, opportunities, and stretch assignments. Perhaps more importantly, it boosts confidence in a way that hierarchy usually doesn't.

As the next generation becomes business owners, they are increasingly turning their backs on conventional management wisdom. It may look odd to many, but both studies and stories are showing that moving away from traditional hierarchy increases the odds of business success by increasing employee trust and decreasing employee fear.

Personal Financial Risk

Which is not to say that business can be fear-free. There will always be things to be fearful of, probably starting with keeping your job and, relatedly, standard of living. The American standard of living usually matches — if not exceeds — income. Each successive promotion and raise is an opportunity to increase our standard of living. Rather than viewing this cash infusion as an opportunity to build a buffer, we often just keep treading water.

This is illustrated by the chart below showing that nearly 60% of Americans spend all of — if not more than — their annual income. Even the 60–80% quintile group is not operating at a large enough buffer to give themselves the opportunity to take some personal risks with their career.

There is a reason that many organizations include a credit report or financial history in hiring decisions. They understand that employees with a strained personal financial situation could be tempted to make some disastrous business decisions, if not outright fraud, to get themselves out from financial difficulties.

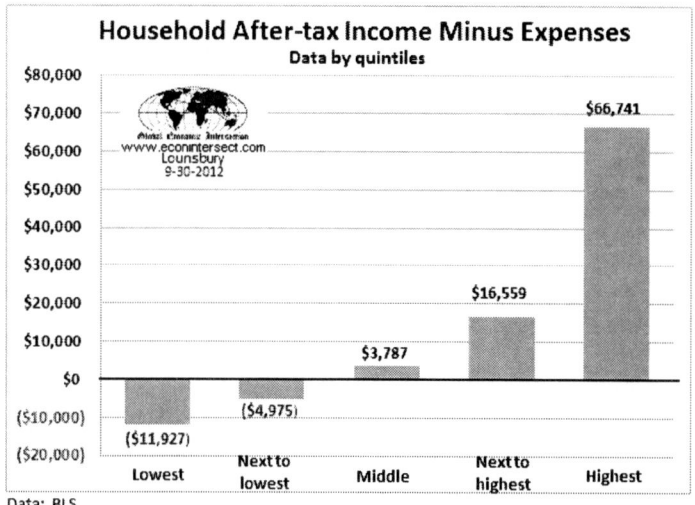

Household After-tax Income Minus Expenses
Data by quintiles

Data: BLS

As a result, most employees' number one priority is to keep their job. This mentality shapes every decision they make and, thus, every decision made in the organization. In many cases, this means making risk-averse decisions, such as not challenging a superior's closely held belief. You've probably done it. I certainly have. It's not bad in and of itself, but sometimes it can lead to worse consequences in the long run.

A personal example. At the insurance company, we once sold gap insurance. If you've purchased a car using a loan, you've been offered gap insurance. It protects the loan borrower against lost equity after driving the car off the lot.

The insurance company hopes there are no negative economic shocks in the aftermarket, like high gas prices decreasing SUV resale value. When those events happen, the insurer can suffer significant losses. If managed properly, though, gap insurance can be profitable.

In the mid-2000s, our company had been on the wrong

end of the gap insurance market and lost millions of dollars. Despite a fast exit, scars from that experience lasted quite awhile. Several years later, a few new managers, lacking that painful history, suggested re-entering the gap insurance market as an expansion opportunity. Considering the more stable market, their suggestion was a good strategic concept. Lingering scars, however, prevented anyone from championing the idea, fearing for their own careers.

Consistent with Anderson and Brown's research, managers avoid making decisions, offering a dissenting opinion, or pushing their ideas forward out of a fear that their suggestion or decision will be seen as too risky. They consider anything other than a textbook answer liable to hurt their future prospects or general standing with managers and executives.

In her book *Daring Greatly*, Brené Brown talks about a conversation she had with Kevin Surace, CEO of Serious Materials and *Inc. Magazine*'s 2009 Entrepreneur of the Year. She asked him what the most significant barrier was to creativity and innovation. His answer is consistent with how our personal fears hold us back in a corporate context:

> I don't know if it has a name, but honestly, it's the fear of introducing an idea and being ridiculed, laughed at, and belittled. If you're willing to subject yourself to that experience, and if you survive it, then it becomes the fear of failure and the fear of being wrong. People believe they're only as good as their ideas and that their ideas can't seem too "out there" and they can't "not know" everything. The problem is that innovative ideas often sound crazy and failure and learning are part of revolution. Evolution and

incremental change is important and we need it, but we're desperate for real revolution and that requires a different type of courage and creativity.

The real problem with this fear is that most companies truly believe they foster innovation. If asked, they would likely say that taking risks is important for innovation. They might even say — and believe — that they foster risk-taking towards innovation. However, the disconnect between this perception — how they say they value risk-taking — and the reality — that people fear losing opportunities and their jobs — could not be more obvious.

According to Lisa Bodell and Ron Ashkenas, writing in the *Harvard Business Review*, "The reality in many organizations today is that despite the public emphasis on innovation, the underlying culture may be strongly risk-averse." They outline four ways to be explicit about what risk-taking really means inside your organization.

- Publicly define a smart risk — The better innovation companies distinguish the areas where risk is encouraged, and where it is not. For example, paying customer business may not be the best places to take risks with innovation, but dedicating resources for an internal team to discover new solutions to customer problems might be.

- Use the right words to encourage the right culture — For example, using terms like "experiment" or "scouting mission," instead of "successful vs. unsuccessful project," will signal a more open attitude toward risk.

- Keep it nimble and small — Size matters, and when it comes to innovation risk, smaller — and faster — experiments are often better.

- Establish clear phases and criteria for funding.

Another way that individual fears play into behavior at work is how we work for our managers. With the knowledge that a manager or executive is expecting or hoping for a certain outcome, it's easy to focus on a single data point to the detriment of the larger project, plan, or vision.

As an operations executive at the insurance company, I had the misfortune of watching this play out to disastrous proportions. My division sold an insurance product that had gotten swept up into the larger mortgage crisis of the Great Recession. As a result, there was extra scrutiny.

From a fear of headlines and regulatory action, the Board of Directors forced us to self-report a regulatory problem before being able to quantify the issue and without a clear timeline for remediation. The senior executives responsible reported weekly to the North American head of insurance and the Board of Directors, able only to focus on a few data points rather than broader implications.

As a result, most resources were marshaled to increase one specific indicator a percentage point or two. Meanwhile, many issues were bubbling just below the surface — team morale, client issues, and even other key indicators — and were being ignored in order to show a good headline number.

This was convenient for all parties involved. For management, it was easier to narrow the problem than to deal with complexity in a holistic way. With quick figures and soundbites, they had the possibility of sounding good in front of executives and board members. Executives and directors tend to like that approach as well. They can believe they are doing their job and provide accountability without spending more money or getting more involved.

The result, however, masks the real problem until it blows up into a major issue. But a manager, knowing they will encounter too many questions that aren't "defensible" in their cultural context, makes the safe choice — and the wrong decision.

These managerial fears can play out across the entire business world — and very recently has in a financial context. As a response to the Great Recession, companies began hoarding cash. Not necessarily out of good sound financial management, but because captains of industry aren't terribly different from everyone else. In response to scars, they become risk-averse.

Financial managers who have gone through a soul-searing downturn — such as what we saw during the 2007–09 bear market — have a special reverence for cash. A 2013 *USA Today* article notes the prevalence of this fear-based decision-making:

> We find that CEOs who were previously employed at a firm that experienced financial difficulties have a cash-to-assets ratio that is 3.1 to 4.4 percentage points higher compared to firms whose CEOs did not experience financial difficulties," Dittmar and Duchin write.

> Companies overall in 1980 had $234.6 billion cash, adjusted for inflation, according to a paper by Amy

Dittmar at the University of Michigan's Stephen M. Ross School of Business and Ran Duchin at the University of Washington's Michael G. Foster School of Business. That's about 12% of assets. Cash holdings grew to $1.5 trillion, or 22% of assets, in 2011. You could make the argument that managements with lots of cash that only increase dividends or buy back shares are simply fearful and lazy, and more concerned with their stock price than with growing their core business.

In short, there's a broad fear of risk-taking that comes from mistrust among teammates, peers, and management, mistrust in organizational structures themselves, and personal financial concerns. Failure is deeply feared. And it's hurting businesses across the country.

Fear of Failure

When AG Lafley recently re-took the helm of Procter & Gamble after some questionable business decisions by the previous CEO, he was quoted by *The Business Journals* as saying, "If you watch human behavior, it's hard for people to make choices, and particularly hard to make choices in the face of uncertainty. That's, frankly, the daily condition of business, especially in a more globally competitive economy."

This is someone who knows what it means to provide leadership in the face of risk. He isn't paralyzed by the fear of failure but rather has the confidence in his leadership abilities and seizes the opportunity to make decisions.

The truth is, failure can be a necessity for true success for many individuals. As a very practical example, author JK Rowling of *Harry Potter* fame said this about her personal failures:

Ultimately, we all have to decide for ourselves what constitutes failure, but the world is quite eager to give you a set of criteria if you let it. So I think it fair to say that by any conventional measure, a mere seven years after my graduation day, I had failed on an epic scale. An exceptionally short-lived marriage had imploded, and I was jobless, a lone parent, and as poor as it is possible to be in modern Britain, without being homeless. The fears that my parents had had for me, and that I had had for myself, had both come to pass, and by every usual standard, I was the biggest failure I knew.

Now, I am not going to stand here and tell you that failure is fun. That period of my life was a dark one, and I had no idea that there was going to be what the press has since represented as a kind of fairy tale resolution. I had no idea then how far the tunnel extended, and for a long time, any light at the end of it was a hope rather than a reality.

So why do I talk about the benefits of failure? Simply because failure meant a stripping away of the inessential. I stopped pretending to myself that I was anything other than what I was, and began to direct all my energy into finishing the only work that mattered to me. Had I really succeeded at anything else, I might never have found the determination to succeed in the one arena I believed I truly belonged. I was set free, because my greatest fear had been realized, and I was still alive, and I still had a daughter whom I adored, and I had an old typewriter and a big idea. And so rock bottom became the solid foundation on which I rebuilt my life.

The benefits of failure have been studied more academically, too. In the *Journal of Personality and Social Psychology*, Joachim Brunstein and Peter Gollwitzer summarize the prevailing research on failure's impacts on achievement — essentially, that it's essential:

> Wortman and Brehm (1975) suggested that responses to repeated failures need to be seen from a time course perspective. Individuals may fight back in the face of initial failures in a reactive attempt to reestablish control. Also, Ford and Brehm (1987) argued that prior failure may lead to perception of a subsequent task as comparatively more difficult. Because more difficult tasks commonly elicit more effort than easy tasks — at least up to a certain point (Wright & Brehm, 1989) — this may result in enhanced effort expenditure on the subsequent task.

> But even among individuals working on one and the same task, the experience of setbacks may stimulate effort and foster performance. According to Carver and Scheier's (1990, 1991; Carver, Blaney, & Scheier, 1979) theorizing, failure feedback induces a discrepancy between a desired outcome (standard or reference value) and the status quo (input). Given

that the expectation of achieving the desired outcome is high, individuals will renew their efforts and thus try to produce outputs that meet the reference value.

In short, people don't like failing, but failing can make people work harder toward success. Even among businesspeople, there's a basic recognition that a failure-allowing culture is a key building block for greatness. A 2012 survey of Inc. 500 CEOs asked, "Which factors contribute to your company's ability to innovate?" After obvious answers about recruiting and retaining talented people, the highest response — with a 61% response rate — was "Creating an environment in which it's OK to fail."

If failure is supposedly so beneficial, why is it so rarely tolerated? Quite simply because of fear. All the previously mentioned components of fear, from the personal all the way up to the structural, prevent organizations from being willing to take the very risks that provide the learning environments necessary for growth, breakthroughs, and success beyond typical market performance.

Which is not to say that no company has ever created an environment that allows failure. Some have done it, fostering a culture that allows people to fail in a way that doesn't kill the company. One such example is the Mickey Drexler-run J. Crew. To underscore how this attitude has had such a positive impact on the results of the company, look at the profile of Drexler in *Fast Company*:

> Before Drexler came to J Crew designers were
> ordered to develop products that would meet specific
> merchandising goals. "We were told we need this
> bucket and this bucket," says J Crew head of women's

design Tom Mora. "I need a merino sweater that is $48 that has a stripe." And you are jamming your design into that bucket and that's what you get a design in a bucket. Drexler told Lyons not only to scrap the buckets but also she says, "Don't tell me what you're doing, don't show any of the merchants, just go and do it and then show me." In generating those designs, Lyons' style and manner give her staff implicit permission to take risks.

Under Drexler and Lyons, J. Crew would become a company of constant and freewheeling experimentation, iteration, adaptation. When experiments don't work out as well, all Lyons requires is for her staff to assume responsibility.

Google is another fantastic example of how to create a culture that allows failure. While somewhat more complex than J. Crew, Google still shares the same hopes of creating the breakthrough technologies and product innovations that will propel the business into future revenue streams and competitive advantages. Google refers to these efforts as "moonshots" — innovations 10x greater than anything else in the marketplace.

Google and J. Crew both understand that enduring companies are built over long periods of time, not quarter-to-quarter. As such, they have a built-in capability to deal with short-term failure. But when companies focus on how to incrementally improve core products for immediate improvements, their myopic view of innovation prevents them from making real breakthroughs. Like the ones from Google's moonshot approach: "Guys like Larry (Page) don't focus on preserving value; they just work on building new value."

Which sounds fine when you have tens of billions of dollars to spend on innovation and create many expensive flops. But, let's be honest, it can't work for all companies. Still, the mindset is an important one. Important enough to find a way to make it work. Practically, even Google takes a rational approach. They don't just throw billions of dollars at a given category, as noted in a *Time* profile:

> Page has also concentrated on avoiding flops like Wikipedia knockoff Knol and Google Buzz, a Twitter clone almost nobody wanted to use. He has done this in part by ratcheting down the number of new product introductions and axing existing projects in period "spring cleanings." He has in a memorable phrase, declared his intention to put "more wood behind fewer arrows."

What's important to note is that he's still bravely putting wood behind arrows. Not fearing the loss of wood.

The Essex Revisited

As the *Essex* and its crew zeroed in on the whale that was ultimately their undoing, frustration was growing. *In the Heart of the Sea* describes the internal conflict:

> Mates became so disgusted with their boatsteerers' unsuccessful attempts to harpoon whales that they ordered them aft and took the iron themselves. One mate, Comstock, screamed, "Who are you? What are you? Miserable trash, scum of Nantucket, a whimpering boy from the chimney corner. By Neptune I think you are afraid of a whale." When the

boatsteerer finally burst into tears, the mate ripped the harpoon from his hands and ordered him to take the steering oar

With the crew demoralized, two attempts to spear the giant whale led to damaged boats. In the chaos aboard the *Essex*, attempting to repair the boats put men out of position: a younger hand steering the *Essex* itself. Too close to the massive whale, the *Essex* itself was soon torn apart.

I realize that's a whaling ship from the 1800s — a far different situation than a modern-day business. Ultimately, though, it was still a failure of leadership. Captain Pollard didn't set the tone, didn't train and coach, didn't empower the crew, and didn't make strong decisions in the moment:

Pollard had known better, but instead of pulling rank and insisting that his officers carry out his proposal to sail for the Society Islands, he embraced a more democratic style of command. Modern survival psychologists have determined that this "social" — as opposed to "authoritarian" — form of leadership is ill suited to the early stages of a disaster, when decisions must be made quickly and firmly.

We all know Captain Pollards and the leadership vacuum created by their inability to truly lead. It undid the *Essex*, and it can undo any organization.

A quick recap of the fear factors around management and decision-making:

1. **Mistrust** — Mistrust can disrupt an organization's by driving a wedge between employees and between employees and management. We highlighted a few such as executive pay and management quality. The

end result is a toxic mix of paranoia and fear, preventing organizations from achieving greatness.

2. **Organizational hierarchies** — Combined with other fear factors such as bad managers, steep hierarchical structures can both decrease effectiveness and increase mistrust and fear in an organization.

3. **Personal fears** — With many Americans using their entire incomes on lifestyle rather than building up cash reserves, they don't feel the freedom to take career risks. This can affect not just how managers make decisions, but also how they inform executives tying to make even larger decisions.

4. **Fear of failure** — When organizations implicitly tell people that failure is not an option, opportunities for breakthroughs vastly decline.

5
FEAR INDICATOR 2
– INDIVIDUALITY

"I've gotten used to [walking in heels like this]. When people talk about me as a Wall Street, stiletto-wearing chick... the stiletto part is right, but I really don't consider myself Wall Street. I take pride in being an industrialist. I understand that people write about what I wear and what I look like because it's an anomaly. But to only focus on those things is to really miss who I am. I'm trying to show women that they need to be women in a man's world."

— Lynn Tilton, CEO Patriarch Partners

I HAVE TYPICALLY WORKED in very buttoned-down, conservative corporate cultures: accounting firm Arthur Andersen, a large super-regional bank, and an insurance company that sold insurance to banks. I developed a definitive view of corporate culture prior to taking my current role as the Director of Finance for a young, new media company named Epipheo.

During my first week at Epipheo, I had my kids in the office. There's a pool table, indie music in the background, writers slouching on sofas, and other stuff that you might associate with Silicon Valley, not Corporate America. As important clients and business partners were visiting soon, I found myself struggling with how the place should look and feel.

I spoke with a salesperson preparing for the visit. He shared my concern, saying that he didn't want them to think we were just a frat house pretending it could play with the big boys.

Despite these insecurities, I realized that we aren't pretending at all. We simply are who we are — and that can be refreshing. Each time a CMO or a product specialist visits, they find a culture that values life integration, unique talents, and a comfortable workspace. More importantly, they find the culture to be a breath of fresh air, communicating that we think a little differently about business. This also communicates that we can think differently about their product and convey their value in a way that resonates with their customers. Better than a more traditional agency and often times better than their in-house marketing teams.

This cultural identity might sound natural, but we have to fight to maintain it. We do so largely by regularly ensuring that individuals don't feel the pressure to conform. Individualism, in fact, shapes any organizational identity, so creating a healthy way for individuals to contribute unhindered is a key to establishing a brave culture.

The notion that we could lose our own individuality through our business organizations may sound silly. However, in organizations both big and small, we risk losing who we are — organizationally and individually — when we craft our messages and actions to fit the expectations of those who manage and lead us.

Covering Individuality

Such a loss of individuality happened during my time at the insurance company. After a couple years from my move out of Internal Audit and into a line of business, I was given responsibility for a service center of about 100 employees. The unit had been around for over twenty years, and its established culture was equal parts entrepreneurial and dysfunctional.

To assess strengths and weaknesses, I wanted to get a first-hand perspective of where talent may have been hiding, or not. I quickly threw myself into understanding the managers and supervisors. Within that group, two young women were frustrated with the leadership for not providing more opportunities.

They seemed capable, but I wanted to speak to others who had experience with them. I encountered a common refrain — their appearance. That they wore all black. Or that their clothes didn't fit well. I was astounded that talk of their appearance dominated their performance discussions. I soon found that many other women had had this same experience, feeling as though their personal style was the main discussion about their employment.

Unconcerned with their fashion, I gave the two women more opportunities. They excelled.

Too many coaching and mentoring conversations begin with superficial considerations. Besides being demoralizing for the people contributing at a high level, they sabotage culture. Especially in corporate America, there's a desperate need for diversity rather than people who all fit a mold. Superficial considerations like fashion are often quick to destroy unique contributions that individuals can deliver.

In 2013, Deloitte released a research paper entitled "Uncovering talent: A new model of inclusion." It provides detailed analytics on the concept of "covering," a term used to describe how even individuals with known stigmatized identities made a "great effort to keep the stigma from looming large." The report identifies that nearly a full two-thirds of all employees in a corporate setting are covering for some aspect — appearance, affiliation, advocacy, or association — of their authentic self and shielding it from those they work with, for, or around. As for notions that covering is only a minority group issue? The report notes that 45% of straight white men reported covering some aspect of their authentic self.

It's not merely a peer issue. 53% of respondents indicated that they felt their leaders expected employees to cover some aspect of their authentic self. Half of those people indicated it affected their level of commitment to the organization.

This desire to cover some aspect of your true self isn't just an issue for individual employees and their ability to feel comfortable within the organization and ultimately less fearful. It can have a profound affect on corporate performance. The *Harvard Business Review* published an article by Dorie Clark, a Duke University marketing professor, entitled "Help Your Employees Be Themselves at Work." About the results of covering, she says:

> High performing companies recognize that diverse
> perspectives can strengthen their performance, and

that homogeneity can cause blind spots (as with a team of right-handed YouTube engineers who realized 10% of videos were being uploaded upside-down because they hadn't considered how left-handed users would maneuver their phones). But in order to unlock the benefits of diversity, we have to make it safe for employees to "uncover" and bring their full selves to work.

A culture of covering also hinders managers from giving constructive feedback. Having seen poor feedback modeled on them, they often think that superficial considerations are valid and even useful pointers. And yet they're surprised when employees don't respond well to feedback that's superficial, not useful for career growth and personal development.

This contrast between the perceptions and expectations of management and employees is highlighted by this graphic from the *Harvard Business Review*:

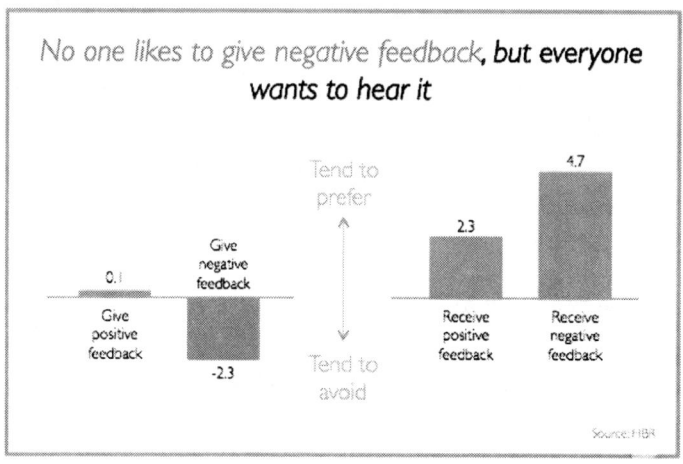

Employees want feedback that can lead to improved performance, but managers' fears stand in the way. Anxiety around performance feedback even enables cultural rot. With a fear of being unable to function without an "expert," managers don't address behavior that negatively affects both culture and performance.

Structures and Individuality

While it's easy and common to unintentionally repress individual expression, there are simple and subtle ways for organizations to promote individuality — and, in turn, improve culture. Structural elements, for example, can encourage individuality to not only be present but rewarded. At Epipheo, we have a Facebook group affectionately termed the Watercooler. It's not controlled, it's not moderated, and it's open to any sort of post, relevant or silly, thought-provoking or mindless. While it could be considered a waste of time — I know I'm guilty — we get participation rates that other companies would envy. It's a pretty good hallmark of individuals feeling comfortable with the culture. And while the posts can be a little off-beat, they often help me understand different creative or focus areas and how their roles are important to the broader context of being successful in the marketplace.

Using technology can reveal more about individuals within an organization and give everyone the opportunity to have an equal voice. Surprising opportunities and innovations can surface and earn resources. Conversations can operate on a shared baseline when everyone has seen a video or article being referenced.

In our case, the Facebook platform has been widely successful in getting people to see communications. This is in stark contrast to what I have seen in more corporate environments where intranets are hidden behind multiple security features. At a previous employer, the intranet required an additional login after logging into the network. As a result, under half of the company ever used it.

Despite the very obvious benefits of using open technology to spread culture, fearful companies are too afraid of employees' authentic selves to relinquish control. There are even many examples of using technology to thwart individual expressions.

When I was in IT Audit, I helped review a technology for monitoring company email. While there may be some very valid reasons for email monitoring — for instance, ensuring it's not being used to view or disseminate sexually explicit material that's either illegal or harassment — I'm not looking debate the intended merits. Rather, I want to talk about unintended consequences.

After scanning our network for two weeks, the potential vendor presented a report. It focused on discussions of violence and sex, unsurprisingly, but also résumés, and competitors' names. The intent was to help monitor policy adherence, but the underlying premise was clearly distrust.

Not wanting to feel obligated to act on the information or be liable for not acting, the CIO decided not to get the technology. Even still, I often had to dispel notions that the company was monitoring email. And no wonder everyone thought so. The last extensive research found that approximately 75% of companies use email monitoring technologies. Just another indicator of how little trust employees have in their company's management.

Email monitoring isn't the only tool that creates individual fear. My sister-in-low once received a LinkedIn message from a former co-worker who was considering leaving the company. He had questions about what happened with some of her benefits so he could make a decision about when to tender his resignation. The next day, his manager fired him. They'd been monitoring his LinkedIn account.

Whether this sort of monitoring is warranted or not, the stories of it breed fear. Employees assume they are being monitored and filter their communications because of it. Regardless of actual monitoring activity, their assumptions contribute to a corporate culture of fear. Companies know they need fresh ideas to remain competitive, but their fear-based surveillance quashes the individuality that, if free, could yield such ideas.

While there has been little research in this area of work, Daniel M. Cable of the London Business School, Harvard professor Francesca Gino, and UNC's Brad Staats studied this aspect of work culture at an Indian call center that was struggling with high burnout. The researchers theorized that part of the reason for the turnover was an adverse reaction to the values instilled during the company's orientation and training systems. Most notably, the Indian workers were urged to adopt Western accents, effectively saying that their individuality was not only unimportant, but even undesirable.

To better understand whether supporting individuality or imposing a sense of authority led to higher performance, the researchers tried setting up two different orientation systems in the existing one's place.

One program focused on the individual employees, including a one-hour program that probed the newcomers about their individual skills and work experiences. At the end, each employee was given a company fleece labeled with his or her individual name. The second orientation system featured company leaders speaking about the organization's history and values. Employees were given badges with the company's name.

The results? The orientation group that placed a premium on individuality increased retention by 47.2% and was 26.7% less prone to turnover than the orientation group that focused on the company. Meanwhile, customers reported higher satisfaction with the employees who had been through the first, employee-centric orientation.

To borrow from Aretha Franklin, they just want a little respect. How much respect employees feels — not just among peers, but also from managers — affects how engaged they are. A *Harvard Business Review* chart shows it well:

Organizations even stifle individuality after employment ends. Once reserved for employees on the front lines of sales, business development, or account management, non-compete agreements can suppress individuality for years to come.

In late 2014, NPR ran a story about the proliferation of non-competes, interviewing Orly Lobel, a professor at the University of San Diego School of Law and author of the book *Talent Wants To Be Free*:

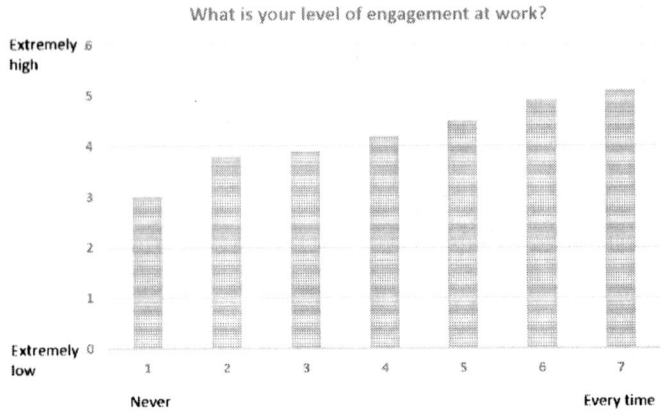

What is your level of engagement at work?

"Part of the reason for the expansion of these agreements is a shift in business culture. Today, it's really human capital that is what creates value," Lobel says. "And companies have this impulse that the way they're going to keep people is by cutting off their outside opportunities."

Non-competes are just the latest mistrust between employees and employers — and they're part of an employee's first impression of the company and its culture. Because of the excitement around a new job, most new hires move past the agreement quickly, but it says something very fearful about what the company thinks about them as an individual.

It also says that the company believes the larger value transfer is from them to the individual, not vice versa. The contributions and unique talents are implicitly undercut. So even if a non-compete isn't an explicit attempt to suppress individuality, it still communicates an organization's fear of individuality, even outside of its confines. The non-compete becomes yet another way the fear cycle plays out as those with a feeling of ownership feel the need to control and the cycle of fear continues.

In short, whether it's superficial feedback, surveillance technology, or non-compete clauses, many staples of company culture act to suppress individuality, thwarting the emergence of fresh ideas and diverse insights.

Cultural Fit

But this isn't just management repressing the individuality of rank and file employees. The same thing can happen to managers. The pressure of possible failure, the fear of what an executive might say or think, concerns about media exposure or regulatory actions — these can all put managers in a place where they have lost their individuality and make decisions without tapping into their unique talents and perspectives.

To use sports as a business analogy, coaches are very similar to managers. Colin Cowherd of ESPNRadio was talking about two coaches — Rex Ryan and Lane Kiffin — who weren't living up to expectations or their own gusto. He pointed out how their individuality seemed stifled:

> [Rex Ryan] clearly is OK'ing things before he
> says anything in the press. I never thought Rex
> was supposed to be a head coach. He is a heck of
> a defensive coach. I don't see him as a 2013 NFL
> coach. Maybe he will turn it around. But it's weird,
> if you're going to go down in life in a job or in a

professional career, you want to do it, as a guy, your way. Maybe that's too guy-ish or too testosterone. But Lane Kiffin came to USC cocky, a risk-taker, he has become afraid of coaching, he coaches scared. He's coaching scared. He was a huge risk-taker. There was a lot of bravado. So it offended people? Who cares! Can't live your life being worried about who you're offending. And Kiffin now is the opposite of the Kiffin that I watched three years ago. He is coaching scared, He's coaching not to lose. That's not who you are, that's not your identity. At Tennessee he took gambles, at USC he took gambles, at Oakland he was defiant against Al Davis. That's who he is. Now he's saying we're going to be boring that's who we are. But you're not!"

Not due to any comments made by Cowherd, Lane Kiffin was fired from USC shortly thereafter.

Contrast Kiffin's situation at USC with Pete Carroll and his tenure at the Seattle Seahawks, Going into his third season with the Seahawks, clinging to his job after two losing seasons, Carroll knew a third consecutive losing season would likely be his last. Still, he was bold. He chose an undersized rookie quarterback over an experienced free agent signed to a big deal. CBS Sports.com had this to say about Carroll's gamble:

This move wasn't just a shock to people outside of Seattle. It was *dangerous*. If it backfires, a coach can get fired. And Pete Carroll, he wasn't doing so great at Seattle in August 2012. The easiest thing for Pete Carroll to do in August 2012 would've been to miss the unconventionally obvious — that the little rookie was the best quarterback on the field — and to give the job to the top-dollar free agent, Flynn, signed to be the quarterback. Carroll doesn't do the conventional, though. His way works because it's his way and he believes in it and transfers that belief to everyone around him, and he believed in Russell Wilson before hindsight made that easy.

That hindsight? Refers to how Carroll, the Seahawks, and the undersized QB Russell Wilson won the Super Bowl.

Most of us have examples of managers hiding who they are, missing out on opportunities. Like not connecting with teams in a meaningful way. Being too hesitant to engender a deeper level of commitment and buy-in. Being influenced by what other managers might think. Shying away from making the right decisions for fear of the implications. Whatever the situation, it doesn't take long for managers to become someone other than themselves — and, ultimately, ineffective.

At the end of the day, the thing that kills individuality is fear. Fear of what someone else is going to think about who we are, how we act and the things that we love. This fear creeps in at an early age for most humans, and unless you work hard to combat it in your corporate culture, you risk your entire organization becoming someone else.

I know you've been thinking it. That individuality sounds good as a theory, but that it sometimes isn't good in practice. And you're correct. Finding the right fit between individuals and organizations is crucial.

In Cincinnati, you can't avoid Procter & Gamble. Their high-profile corporate headquarters has cemented Cincinnati as a consumer marketing and branding hub. Within the broader community, P&G employees are often known as Proctoids for their cookie-cutter personality. There is no denying that P&G understands the power of a cultural fit.

As a soon-to-be college graduate, I twice experienced this process. First, pursuing an internship at P&G during my junior year. The process included written tests, surveys, and interviews. I was ultimately rejected. Second, interviewing for a full-time position. Again, I was subjected to a battery of tests and interviews.

Considering that I was still in college, they invested an awful lot of time and effort on me — twice. Clearly, a cultural fit was crucial. Their primary motivation is performance, but the byproduct is a culture that doesn't have to worry about individuality because there is a pre-selected alignment between personal and organizational values.

P&G is willing to make this massive investment because they understand that a bad fit leads to unhappy employees and a poor representation of the brand. They understand that it is not only important to ensure that the individual isn't just technically capable of fulfilling the job responsibilities, but also eager to contribute to the culture and the mission of the company.

However, the idea of cultural fit should be balanced with a healthy separation between work and self. When companies make others feel valued for their differences, not uncomfortably conscious of them, they allow employees to make space between their work and personal lives, fostering a willingness to offer ideas and a desire to improve performance.

In the previous chapter, I mentioned the impact of personal financial fears. A threat to individuality can have the same effect. When employees, lacking a buffer between work and personal lives, begin to see their career as their identity, the stakes become higher at work — perhaps too high for them to act rationally, let alone bravely.

The Essex Revisited

In many organizations, leaders create an environment that can oftentimes quash not only our ability to be ourselves, but also our ability to make our best contributions. The *Essex* was no different. According to *In the Heart of the Sea*, the first mate (second in command) created such a culture:

Nickerson and his Nantucket friends may have thought they knew Chase prior to their departure, but they now realized that, as another young Nantucketer had discovered, "at sea, things appear different." The mate of a Nantucket whaleship routinely underwent an almost Jekyll-and-Hyde transformation when he left his island home, stepping out of his mild Quaker skin to become a vociferous martinet. And so Nickerson saw Owen Chase change from a perfectly reasonable young man with a new wife named Peggy to a bully who had no qualms about using force to obtain obedience and who swore in a manner that shocked these boys who had been brought up, for the most part, by their mothers and grandmothers. "[A]lthough but a few hours before I had been so eager to go [on] this voyage," Nickerson remembered, "there [now] seemed a sudden gloom to spread over me. A not very pleasing prospect [was] truly before me, that of a long voyage and a hard overseer.

It was obvious that the crew's and Nickerson's morale was

impacted by their inability to be themselves, most definitely contributing to the extent of the disaster.

A quick recap of the fear factors around individuality:

Covering. Superficial measures of success can lead to covering, preventing businesses from giving feedback that improves performance and from tapping into real talents and fresh ideas.

Structures. Non-compete clauses, surveillance technology, and fear of criticism make employees and managers alike restrict their individuality as a measure of self-protection. Such a culture impacts management's vision, conviction, and decision-making, rendering organizational execution ineffective.

Cultural fit. A clear and compelling mission, vision, and values are important for any organization to inform the individuality of the organization. A clearly defined and well-known cultural identity can help managers determine the fit of prospective employees and allow them to understand if they can be successful in that culture. This cultural fit impacts your ability to play to your strengths.

6

FEAR INDICATOR 3 - CORPORATE POLITICS

"A good leader can engage in debate frankly and thoroughly, knowing that at the end he and the other side must be closer, and thus emerge stronger. You don't have that idea when you are arrogant, superficial, and uninformed."

— Nelson Mandela

IT'S HARD TO define corporate politics, but, as Supreme Court Justice Potter Stewart famously declared about pornography, "I know it when I see it." And chances are you do too, especially if you've lived through or been the unfortunate victim of corporate politics.

Politics in general is the fight for power or control over a limited set of resources or influence. As more and more groups and interests fight for those resources, the more political maneuvering tends to occur.

A fight for power or influence isn't all bad. What matters is how the struggle plays out and the manner in which people conduct themselves. That is why corporate culture is so important. It can prevent the struggle over resources from being destructive.

Corporate politics — which has many shades and definitions — often creates a culture that is ever-fearful. Not knowing someone's motivations or getting the impression that someone on the team is serving their own interests — perhaps at your expense — can be a killer.

A great case study is, surprise surprise, the US political system. In the 1800s, politics was an artful game played by honorable men referred to as statesmen. Today, well, we usually have other names for our politicians. What changed can be very instructive about how to guard our corporate cultures today.

Let's go back to Daniel Webster, Henry Clay, and John C. Calhoun. These three men, eventually known as the Great Triumvirate, represented three geographic regions with very opposed needs and perspectives, like slavery, states' rights, etc. But their opposition to President Andrew Jackson in the late 1820s brought them into a loose alliance against President Jackson's policies. Though they still operated as rivals, they were also able to work together.

In 1857, essayist Edwin P. Whipple noted Henry Clay's unifying power:

> The nature of Clay, without being deficient in force, was plastic and fluid, readily accommodating itself to the moment's exigency. His faculties and passions

seem all to have united in one power of personal impressiveness, bound together discordant interests and antipathies, made itself felt as inspiration equally in Maine and Louisiana, concentrated in itself the enthusiasm of sense for principles, and of sensibility for men; and these, the qualities of a powerful political leader, who makes all the demagogues work for him, without being himself a demagogue.

In Congress as Well as Public, the Center Increasingly Cannot Hold

Ideological scores of senators and representatives based on roll-call votes. Negative numbers represent liberal views and positive numbers conservative views

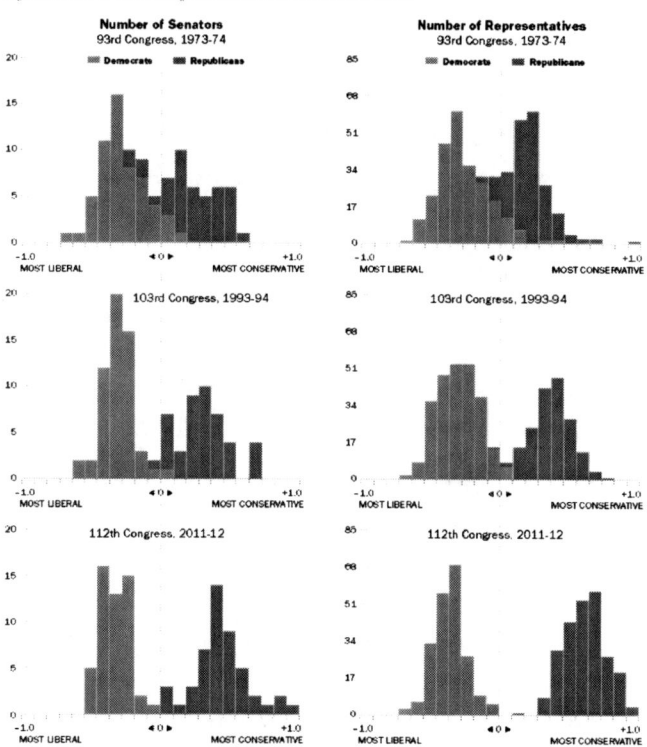

PEW RESEARCH CENTER

Clay, as a politician, strove to be uplifting and driving toward a common good, not divisive.

Today, what with the media always tailored to its ideological audience, we see mostly polarization, not unification. This divide's development is best shown in this *The Economist* infographic of congressional voting records.

While there were clearly differences between the parties in 1989, members of each party still occasionally voted against the party line. By 2013, a very stark division — and even a gap — is obvious.

Our internal organizational politics doesn't work the same way as our political system — thankfully — but we need to be careful to create culture that engenders the Henry Clay type of politics, not the 2013 US Congress. It's important to understand how to resolve competing interests and viewpoints and achieve an end result.

While the perspective of Clay, Calhoun, and Webster was rooted in a greater purpose, the culture in the US has become progressively more selfish and casual. Even their ideas — slavery, states' rights — were broader than contemporary, individualistic talking points. We have clearly defined winners and losers, not compromises or alliances.

This type of politics has become the process of completely devaluing the other side's perspective. If your goal is to completely tear down the other side — to discredit them without offering a viable alternative — it is not politics at all. Instead, it's just a sad attempt to assert some control where none has been earned - a behavior often rooted in the mistrust discussed in Chapter 4.

The unfortunate byproduct of this type of political engagement is what I call the political vortex of fear.

THE POLITICAL VORTEX

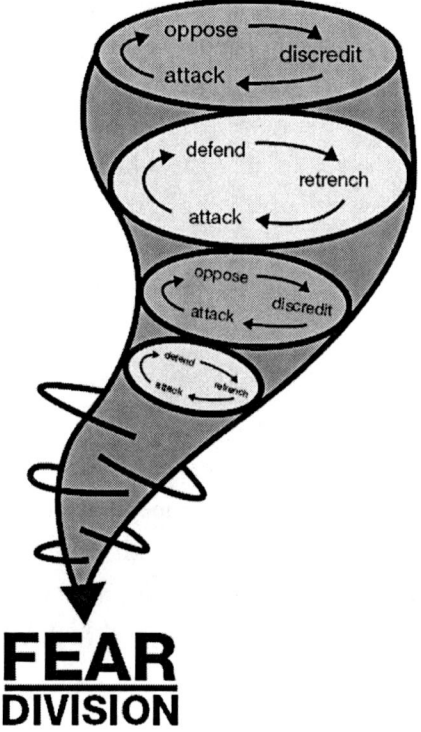

As you can see in the diagram above, the result of this cycle of opposition, discrediting and attacks is a downward spiral with destruction the only thing left in its path.

But when a viable alternative is presented, true politics

can happen. There's negotiation between competing viewpoints and intent to find a solution that works for all parties — because all parties recognize they're part of a single organization. Ultimately, that recognition is the beginning of true — and valuable — corporate politics.

This is exactly how Clay, Calhoun, and Webster established their reputation as great politicians. Even though they had their own important regional issues, they understood that they were a part of something larger — the entire nation. In our own organizations, we have to be careful to remember to focus on the results that the whole company needs, not the smaller issues that can easily consume and polarize us. Perspective is critical!

Lose to Win

In fact, it's often good to "lose" — or provide the appearance of losing — some of those smaller issues. Understanding that there is a larger war and that some conflict points are minor skirmishes, you can build trust with other parties and help retain unity toward larger goals. Plus, in future conflicts, you may be able to negotiate better terms for other priorities.

Shortly after the government shutdown in October 2013, Jack and Suzy Welch wrote an opinion piece on LinkedIn entitled "Schmooze or Lose: How the Lost Art of Negotiation Led to a Shutdown." About the state of politics in the US, the article says:

> You have to schmooze. Clarification: You have to
> schmooze early and often. You can't suddenly burst

out of your office to build relationships when you hear rumbles of trouble from down below, and it's certainly too late by the time a crisis flares. No, schmoozing has to be what you do all the time as a leader; it has to be a massive part of your job. Walking around, having a coffee, sitting and listening, getting real, letting people get real with you. Showing who you are, what you care about, exposing your hopes and dreams and values. Asking people the same about themselves.

Building — in two big fat words — trust and transparency. And look, we're not talking about the standard, ho-ho-ho kind of social schmoozing you do with your customers and your team and your boss. That's easy. That's like President Obama schmoozing with Nancy Pelosi, or John Boehner schmoozing with Eric Cantor.

Leaders have to do something harder and more essential; something that can feel awkward at first. You have to schmooze with your known "adversaries" too, say, for instance, your union, or the group of employees who hate your new strategy and want the old one back. The resistors that exist in every organization. The perennial naysayers. Smart and annoying. Them.

This idea that "schmoozing" can build a bank for when you need to break through tough and competing interests is vitally important to having a political process that is healthy and doesn't destroy a culture. Largely because it builds trust.

In chapter four we talked about the trust, or lack thereof, that exists between a manager and subordinate. As an organization, you must make ways to build trust on a regular basis, because individuals are just not programmed to do this as a normal course of their daily lives. It is difficult and not fun to spend time with someone who disagrees with you, but it's a lot easier when that person has been transparent with you. That common understanding helps you start out tough conversations or struggles for resources not as unknown adversaries but as colleagues who have some trust between them.

But politics isn't just person-to-person. In corporations, it commonly involves third parties like labor unions. This tension between labor and management is a large source of political fear inside organizations, creating mistrust that can have far reaching negative implications on culture.

According to a Gallup poll, only one in five Americans trusts unions the same level as banks or big business. Some of the reasons cited for this mistrust include:

- Unions create an "us versus them" culture within companies instead of putting everyone on the same team.

- They create a culture of entitlement.

- They restrict flexibility and hurt competitiveness.

- They maintain ludicrous compensation and benefit levels for jobs based purely on seniority (some bartenders in a New York hotel union make approximately $200,000 a year, nearly 10 times above the job's average national wage of $21,600).

- They force companies to treat all union employees equally, regardless of the relative skill and value of particular employees, thus reducing incentives for people to do a great job.

The study found that unions have a distinct culture and that the nature of the cultural variation may challenge to a company's well-being:

> The union-non-union relationship can be thought of as a fault-line due to a number of factors including labor-management relations, conflict and differences in the characteristics of the people, job and work context and the fact that union members are usually the only subgroup assessed dues to belong. Each of these factors make it likely that union and nonunion groups will diverge from one another over time, developing at least some values, norms and beliefs/assumptions that are unique.

While I don't intend to imply that all management-union relations behave in this way, this natural tension can be firmly entrenched. A perfect example of this mistrust and fear can be seen in an account from *Bloomberg Business*:

> The SEC's employee union president is warning workers to keep lunch breaks to a half-hour or risk being disciplined as "absent without leave."

> "Despite the fact that most SEC employees are often told that they may take an hour for lunch, technically, we are only entitled to thirty minutes," wrote Greg Gilman, an SEC lawyer who heads the agency's union chapter, in an e-mail sent to colleagues

on Oct. 24. "Do not fall into the trap of believing that because you are a 'professional' the rules do not apply to you." In his message, Gilman cautioned employees to "be careful not to take a walk to get coffee, even with your supervisor," because "a case may be built very easily based upon these types of behaviors."

Fueling the union's angst is an SEC plan requiring the use of security cards to record the times people enter and exit the building in its offices across the country, a move Gilman wrote would "substantially increase surveillance."

Look at the words and phrases used: angst, surveillance, "case may be built," trap, disciplined. Not exactly words or phrases that connote trust or mutual understanding.

Labor unions are not the only place where the level of trust with a third party can determine the level of business success. Suppliers, business partners, and alliance partners can have the same dynamic.

Working in the insurance industry for a decade, I saw this dynamic in agent-company relationships. For historical context, the insurance business was built on the model where policies were purchased through an individual agent. This worked well for decades, since insurance is a complex contract with a delicate balance between coverage and price. Independent agents played an important role as an arbitrator between consumers and the insurance company.

But with the Internet, companies can go directly to the consumer, creating a conflict with the agents they had relied upon for decades. The company I worked for walked that line very delicately. On one hand, we were building a direct-to-consumer portal. On the other hand, we were telling the agents that they were an important part of our business strategy.

Some companies balanced this by continuing to pay their agents a commission, albeit a smaller one, for the customers in their territory who purchased directly. But that can only go on for so long. Eventually, commissions will be phased out or agents will defect to other companies that were truly committed to the agent model.

You can see how this would deeply hinder any real politics from happening, even though the insurance company and the agent both want to sell insurance. The refusal to compromise will itself compromise corporate politics.

Resource Allocation

The political relationships of peers, labor unions and partnerships are important to consider, but even more important is the root of their conflict. In a business context, there's almost always one thing at stake: resource allocation.

And, just as with political relationships, it's important to keep a unified strategy in mind, not get caught up in regional or personal needs or wants. The insurance company I worked for showed me a great example of how politics can go wrong when decision-making isn't linked to the larger corporate strategy.

My last few years there, I ran operations for a division that sold insurance to financial institutions. We were a high-growth division and, despite being in a market with one dominant provider, we had opportunities to consolidate market share from the smallest players and become the second-largest in the industry. One president even made our division a pillar for growth using a cheesy — and arguably non-appropriate — picture of an old temple.

During meetings, everyone in the company would talk about how my division was key to growth and profitability. But when it came time to make actual investments, decisions got trumped by a few key executives who wanted to leverage older, less profitable, and dying parts of the business — even though it conflicted with corporate strategy.

The effects were under-capitalized divisions like mine, infrastructure issues, and lost opportunities. The company lacked the capabilities it needed because politics had steered investment decisions in prior years.

There were many reasons for these decisions (including fear factors from other chapters of this book), but it all could have been prevented if executives had simply been able and willing to follow overarching corporate strategy when making investment decisions.

Executive decisions aren't the only pitfalls to resource allocation. The process itself is often complex, undefined, or misunderstood. Sometimes finance, in an attempt to move the budgeting process along, just dictates to management how much they get rather than working through actual business needs. Often, this occurs because the business plan process isn't linked to the budgeting process, or a business plan hasn't been created with enough detail for finance to link the budgeting process to actual strategies.

Regardless, the key is to ask strategic questions. Is the process and decision-making linked to a larger corporate strategy? More importantly, is it consistent with corporate strategy? Is the process known and easy to navigate? Does the organization see the benefits?

If the answers to these questions are 'no' or 'unknown' then you likely have a resource allocation process that contributes to toxic corporate politics instead of having a corporate political system that is functional and able to accomplish for the business.

If the answer is 'yes' then stick to the process. Unlike with relationships, you can't schmooze resource allocation. Always keeping a focus on corporate strategy will help ensure that corporate politics bring overall gains, not needless conflict or misguided decisions.

Clear, Consistent Communication

As for the corporate political process, it's simple: the process breaks down when there is inconsistency and confusion. And a breakdown of the political process creates fear.

In every organization I have ever been a part of, the employees have always complained about communication. It shows up on internal employee surveys, there are complaints around the water cooler, and executives know it is a common problem. But it seems we refuse to get better at it.

Part of the problem is seeing good communication only as a factor of quantity. When managers hear that there is a communication problem, the tendency is to send out more of it:

more emails, more town hall meetings. But both of these tend to be fairly ineffective. In fact, the increase in volume of communication only serves to increase the perception that communication is getting worse.

But poor communication really means communication that is either lacking or in conflict with the broader corporate messages being sent by the executive team or corporate communications. This sort of communication breeds fear because people instinctively know that they're not being told something.

I experienced this disconnect many times at the insurance company. Prior to acquisition by a larger group, we were a small niche company, still closely owned by the original founding family while also generating $1 billion in annual premiums. The CEO was the grandson of the founder, and he had a real folksy way of connecting with employees. He would regularly walk around the entire campus and personally thank everyone for their hard work.

After the acquisition, communication standards shifted. The new group CEO emailed us in obviously translated English with lots of unfamiliar corporate language. Beyond the style of communication, the concepts themselves seemed designed to confuse. Our long-term profit sharing plan, previously based on a simple three-year average of growth rate and return on beginning equity, was replaced with a plan containing over 25 measures of performance, calculated across four pages of a spreadsheet. Our understanding of our performance and personal financial opportunities disappeared instantly. At the same time, our connection to our division's performance diminished greatly.

Shortly thereafter, our new division executive held an all-day planning session with every manager in the company. (As an aside, having every manager of a $1 billion organization at an off-site is a fantastic way to ensure nothing gets accomplished.) One agenda item was a survey that had indicated our communication as an organization was poor and trending worse. In the conversation, the managers offered suggestions ranging from the CEO blogging more frequently to lunch-and-learns with members of the senior executive team — again, efforts toward volume of top-down communication, not overall quality.

Meanwhile in private conversations, mid-level managers indicated they did not have regular one-on-one meetings with their divisional executive, or that they received no or incomplete performance reviews. Many indicated that the conversations they did have with their executives conflicted with the messages being sent by the CEO.

If management had just looked a little deeper than the surface, they would have understood that it wasn't the quantity of communication, but the nature and inconsistency of the communication.

All employees want their manager to bring bigger organizational decisions down to the level of how these decisions impact daily work. That's it. Personal, consistent communication. They simply want to understand their connection to the organization's purpose. Managers that do this well have high-performing teams and likely have employees that feel communication is clear.

These teams and employees are not confused by how their work matters or fits into the larger context. With an understanding of corporate strategy, these teams and employees can have effective politics and not get sidetracked by small, individual interests. Which, of course, is better for the overall strategy itself.

Beyond Strategy

And yet, sometimes the key to managing corporate politics is seemingly unrelated to corporate strategy.

Consider community service. A 2013 *Time* magazine survey found 42% of Americans had performed no service in the past year and 64% performed service less than a few times per year. Not really surprising when you consider American attitudes toward anything that doesn't fit their lifestyles or bring personal benefit.

But service *is* personally beneficial. Many studies have shown service's positive impacts on the individual serving: perspective on how others live, improved ability to help and work well with other people, increased respect in general.

These same attributes can also be applied in a corporate context and can break down barriers between people and departments that desperately depend on each other to accomplish mutual goals and strategies. Though these barriers are often created as natural boundaries for our teams to function, they can keep others out and create the sort of mistrust that troubles corporate politics. In attempts to create camaraderie within departments, we often create culture at the expense of other departments, even turning them into de facto enemies for being "someone else."

While this sounds harsh, and you may be telling yourself this doesn't happen in your company, think about how often you hear sentiments criticizing other departments. Like, "The sales team is always cutting sweetheart deals." Or, "It's the wild west over there." Or, "I submitted that request, but they never respond in under a month." Among other sarcastic, snide remarks.

Whereas service, precisely because it isn't in a corporate context, can provide opportunities for employees and managers not only to interact with other parts of the organization but also enjoy meaningful interactions.

To take this concept even further, embrace diversity. Not necessarily skin color or gender differences, but rather diversity in the personality, experiences, and skill sets of employees. Those diverse skillsets work together to create a better organization.

Lynda Gratton, a management professor at the London Business School, notes in the *Harvard Business Review* the role of diversity in organizations that have had large public failures in the past couple decades:

> Thinking again about the problems encountered by
> BP, RBS and Nokia in the past decade, as different as
> they were, it's possible to see a common factor. These
> firms lacked diverse, highly collaborative leadership
> teams. At RBS, CEO Fred Goodwin isolated himself
> from his colleagues, failed to listen to others, and
> became increasingly selfish in his behavior. At Nokia,
> the senior leadership team was for a long time
> extraordinarily homogenous (mostly men, mostly
> from Finland, mostly software engineers, mostly

educated in Helsinki). How likely was it that they would be on top of the rapid developments in Asian consumer markets, or in technology and design emanating from Silicon Valley? At BP, we know top management found it difficult to integrate US assets and build collaborative relationships with the leaders of US acquisitions – contributing to a problem with implementing safety standards globally.

Simply put, as businesses are increasingly challenged by dynamic change and crises, it becomes ever more crucial for their leadership teams to have sufficient diversity to see what is happening from different perspectives, and sufficient collegiality to work collaboratively with each other even when under stress.

Again, while you need to keep corporate strategy in mind when making decisions, it's also important to consider how politics might be deeply affected by aspects that are very far from the bottom line. Bravery can come from unexpected places.

The Essex Revisited

What role did politics have on the decisions that led to months adrift at sea, starvation, and death? From *In the Heart of the Sea*, we realize that the politics between the captain and first mate had a huge role in the fear-based decisions that led to ruin.

Chase was fired with more than the usual amount of

ambition and, as he started his third voyage, he made no secret of his impatience to become a captain. "Two voyages are generally considered sufficient to qualify an active and intelligent young man for command," he would write, "in which time, he learns from experience, and the examples which are set him, all that is necessary to be known." He was six years younger than Captain Pollard, but Chase felt he had already mastered everything he needed to know to perform Pollard's job. The first mate's cocksure attitude would make it difficult for Pollard, a first-time captain just emerging from the long shadow of a respected predecessor, to assert his own style of command.

This is but one example of how personal politics can contribute to a dysfunctional organization that gets rocked by fear and loses its way from its real goals.

A quick recap of the fear factors around corporate politics:

1. **Lose to win.** Despite different individual goals, understanding and compromise is required to achieve the more important corporate goals.

2. **Resource allocation.** Corporate politics is a struggle for resources. A lack of clarity on how resources are awarded can lead to fear and mistrust.

3. **Clear, consistent communication.** How precise are the messages from senior management? Do they conflict with lower-level experience? How well can employees understand their daily role?

Communication must be measured by quality, not quantity.

4. **Beyond strategy**. Service and diversity can both help foster a better political process by helping everyone see beyond their immediate interests and "needs."

7
FEAR INDICATOR 4 –
THE COMPETITION

"Guys like Larry (Page) don't focus on preserving value; they just work on building new value."

— Ben Horowitz

AN EPISODE OF the PBS show *Nature* features the constant conflict for survival between wolves and buffalo in the Canadian Wood Buffalo National Park. To take down an animal as much as 20 times their size, the wolves' strategy is to get behind the buffalo and force them to run. As long as the buffalo can keep together, they are safe. But the wolves constantly jockey for position, attempting to isolate a weaker member of the herd. This struggle for position can go on for hours.

If the buffalo maintain their resolve — firm in their

identity as the stronger, more powerful animals — they maintain the safety of the entire herd. But if a member of the herd becomes afraid and scampers away, the advantage shifts to the wolf pack. Their agility, stamina, and numbers can take down the solo buffalo.

This same intricate dance between foes plays out in business. We strive to understand our strengths and weaknesses, our opponents' approach to battle, who has the advantage at any given moment, and how to exploit the advantage when we have it. Even more important than knowing those aspects is keeping everyone focused on them so that fear does not split the herd and give up the organization's advantage.

Know the Competition by Knowing Yourself

Successful businesses never ignore their competition, but they also don't mimic it. Having started successful small businesses, I know it's common to see look-alike businesses trying to compete in the same market. When I notice those businesses, I often have concern or even fear. Worrying about competition is natural, but the key to not falling prey is knowing who you are as a business — including your value proposition, your strengths, and your weaknesses.

When you're secure in your own identity, competition can be good, not just because it spurs you on to greater performance, but because competitors may even boost your reputation. If the competition tackles a part of the market that you've avoided, they can foster positive press about your industry as a whole or raise awareness about your business almost as a partner serving a different segment of the market.

In 2005, my wife and I started BabysitEase, an occasional and part-time child-care service primarily focused on the Cincinnati marketplace. We knew we had a good and unique childcare concept and had some early success. As is the case with most entrepreneurs, we (mostly me) began to develop ambitions, including expansion into other markets.

We joined a nanny association and went to their annual meeting in New Orleans. While there, we quickly realized that we were not only outsiders but were viewed as enemies of the association. Every educational session dealt with the emerging risk of SitterCity, a business similar to our own that had achieved national scale. Speaker after speaker talked about the scourge of SitterCity on the industry, how they would make a legitimate industry an illegitimate industry overnight. Being a company not unlike SitterCity, we stayed quietly in the background. Our takeaway was that we had the potential to be an industry disrupter.

The nanny industry viewed these new babysitting services as something that needed to be stamped out rather than a new market participant reaching out to an underserved population, perhaps even helping improve the perception and growth of the industry.

Despite having a different value proposition from SitterCity and Care.com (list services that still left families doing most of the work of qualifying and scheduling), we embraced them and talked to their founders early on. While we needed to differentiate our service offering from theirs, we viewed their success as a source of legitimacy for our own business. Because our target market had heard of SitterCity and Care.com, they were willing to use us.

Knowing who we are has allowed us to exist within a competitive landscape. While SitterCity and Care.com have earned venture capital funding and now dominate the market, we were content to grow slowly — especially as our family grew quickly. Instead of trying to take control of markets or own the services through a franchise model, we serve existing mom and pop childcare services by licensing our technology and providing our business knowledge. If anything, competition helped us find that niche.

David Goldberg, CEO of SurveyMonkey, praises the same aspects of competition:

> Embrace competition. Don't let competitors keep you from pursuing your idea. Good competitors can help your efforts by laying a foundation of credibility for your product category, help isolate your competitive niche and compel you to bring your best to the marketplace. We often wished we had more competition in my first business because we had to create the market by ourselves.

That said, you ultimately have to focus on your own situation. Brad Field, managing director at the Foundry Group, put it succinctly, "Be obsessively focused on your competitors while ignoring them." In other words, know your rivals' products, market positioning, financial status, and how they engage users, but don't react to every move they make.

In this vein, Amazon's pursuit and purchase of Diapers. com shows the mindset to take. Though some aspects of the acquisition could be seen as fear-driven, Amazon clearly used their unique scale and resources to strike a good balance of monitoring the competition without reacting in a way that would have taken them away from their core identity. As described in *The Everything Store*, they approached it in the following way:

> Focused in part on buying large volumes of merchandise from other online retailers and measuring the quality and speed of their services — how easy it is to buy, how fast the shipping is, and so forth. The mandate is to investigate whether any rival is doing a better job than Amazon and then present the data to a committee of Bezos and other senior executives, who ensure that the company addresses any emerging threat and catches up quickly.

Whether you're Amazon or not, you simply have to run *your* business.

But how do you know what your business really is? It's not just the corporate values published in the cafeteria. It's understanding what has made you successful as an organization and sticking to that value proposition by continuing to enhance it in new and fresh ways that resonate with your customers.

One of the business books most influential on my thinking is a book called *The Discipline of Market Leaders* by Michael Treacy and Fred Wiersema. It was written nearly 20 years ago and includes some dated examples, but its concepts are timeless. On the subject of competition, it focuses on understanding your identity in the marketplace, the pitfalls of confusing that identity, and how to achieve greater and greater performance by embracing your identity in ever greater ways.

The main message is that no company can succeed by trying to be all things to all people. It must instead find the unique value proposition that it alone can deliver to its chosen market. It could have easily been titled *The Discipline to Maintain your Corporate Identity*. Here is an excerpt about using discipline to avoid chasing the competition:

> Many of the ideas you encounter in *The Discipline of Market Leaders* will surprise you. That's because they seem out of step with the current, widely-held notion that to identify core competencies and to reengineer a company's business processes is to assure its competitive future. The flaw in this thinking lies not with the principles and practices of core competencies and reengineering, which are powerful concepts and tools. The flaw lies in the assumption that they are all that an ailing company needs. They are not. Sick or not, if a company is going to achieve and sustain dominance, it must first decide where it will stake its claim in the marketplace and what kind of value it will offer to its customers. Then it can identify core competencies and reengineer the processes that make up the operating model required to get the job done.

The history of American business is littered with examples where fear of the competition has led organizations to copycat products, services, or culture to near-tragic conclusions. Every organization must know its strengths and make decisions about how to compete based on those strengths, not based on the competition's strengths.

Chasing vs. Leading the Market

Being a leading, offensive-minded organization requires that you find advantages giving you a leadership position in the marketplace — a high point or hill that acts as a natural barrier against the invading hoards of the competition.

An "economic moat" — the competitive advantage that one company has over other companies in the same industry — is a term coined by renowned investor Warren Buffett. Investopedia's discussion of the concept says:

> The wider the moat, the larger and more sustainable the competitive advantage. By having a well-known brand name, pricing power, and a large portion of market demand, a company with a wide moat possesses characteristics that act as barriers against other companies wanting to enter into the industry.

In other words, moats give organizations more freedom in the market. But while a competitive moat is nice, what's more important is the mindset it allows. The focus shouldn't be on building a competitive moat but rather on guarding against complacency that can rock you back into a chasing posture or a fear-based mindset. A moat may seem like a defense, but its real value is that it allows you to pursue offensive options.

It is easy to spot companies that are fear-based organizations by how they compete in the marketplace. You can see it in their advertising messages, retail store layouts, or experiences as a customer. When a company defines an aspect of their market, they are a leader and a brave organization. When a company chases the competition rather than leading, they're a fear-based organization.

A good example of a business chasing the competition is McDonald's in the 2000s. From Starbucks and the US's growing cafe culture, McDonald's felt the heat on their breakfast business. In response, the chain toyed with adding dedicated baristas and beverages that sounded similar to Starbucks staples. They even overhauled stores to include things like lounge chairs, electric fireplaces and free Wi-Fi.

A *New York Times* article describes the results:

> But the leisurely cafe culture and the business plan behind fast food are in opposition. Although signs hang in many McDonald's stores instructing customers to spend half an hour or less at the tables, Ms. McComb said there was no national policy about discouraging longtime sitting. "The individual franchisees do what they feel is best for their community businesses."

While McDonald's may have wanted to mimic Starbucks's success at attracting customers willing to spend higher average ticket amounts, they didn't attract that demographic. The people who were attracted to the new stores were "older people seeking company, schoolchildren putting off homework time, and homeless people escaping the cold." Fine groups of customers for an array of reasons — but not for raising average sales.

Another example of an organization that is following instead of leading is Microsoft. Perhaps preposterous that a company with a $345 billion market capitalization (as of Q2 2014) could be fearful of anyone, but they have been playing catch-up to Apple for well over five years.

One way this fear has manifested itself is in its advertising. In response to Apple's popular "Get a Mac" campaign, Microsoft ran several advertising campaigns. First, it ran "I'm a PC," which showed short clips of people, famous and non-famous, proclaiming they are "a PC." Then it ran "Laptop Hunter," which followed someone around looking to buy a new laptop — inevitably settling on a Windows PC.

The "Get a Mac" ads were so popular and effective because they made consumers aspire to get a Mac. When Microsoft's campaigns came as a response, particularly the "Laptop Hunter," they made it seem like shoppers were settling for a PC.

These fear-based ad campaigns are not surprising when you consider that Mark Penn, once a political strategist who worked closely with the Clintons, is Vice President of Advertising and Strategy at Microsoft. The ads had the feel of an attack ad, not a company confident in its strengths.

The same fear characteristics are evident in Microsoft's attempt to create a retail store dedicated to consumer products, mimicking the success of Apple's retail stores. Whereas the typical Apple retail store is bursting with excitement, the Microsoft store, many times located just a few doors down from Apple in the same malls, is often occupied only by sales associates. Rather than drawing away Apple's customers, the store only draws a greater contrast between the companies.

While fear-based cultures respond to the competition, brave cultures lead the market to a new place and capture a position. Such companies have the luxury of a long-term perspective without short-term pressures (see Chapter 4 for more about short-term pressures) and a desire to create a revolutionary step forward as opposed to incremental enhancements to existing products.

Contrarily, Tesla is the quintessential example of a brave company. The actions of Tesla and their founder Elon Musk reflect a truly brave corporate culture. In June 2014, Musk struck what is possibly his bravest action to date: opening his entire patent library, with the only caveat that the technology must be used in good faith. Talk about not fearing competition!

On his blog, Musk writes boldly about competition:

> When I started out with my first company, Zip2, I thought patents were a good thing and worked hard to obtain them. And maybe they were good long ago, but too often these days they serve merely to stifle progress, entrench the positions of giant corporations and enrich those in the legal profession, rather than the actual inventors.

> At Tesla, however, we felt compelled to create patents out of concern that the big car companies would copy our technology and then use their massive manufacturing, sales and marketing power to overwhelm Tesla. We couldn't have been more wrong. The unfortunate reality is the opposite: electric car programs (or programs for any vehicle that doesn't burn hydrocarbons) at the major manufacturers are small to non-existent, constituting an average of far less than 1% of their total vehicle sales.

> At best, the large automakers are producing electric

cars with limited range in limited volume. Some produce no zero emission cars at all.

Given that annual new vehicle production is approaching 100 million per year and the global fleet is approximately 2 billion cars, it is impossible for Tesla to build electric cars fast enough to address the carbon crisis. By the same token, it means the market is enormous. Our true competition is not the small trickle of non-Tesla electric cars being produced, but rather the enormous flood of gasoline cars pouring out of the world's factories every day.

We believe that Tesla, other companies making electric cars, and the world would all benefit from a common, rapidly-evolving technology platform.

Technology leadership is not defined by patents, which history has repeatedly shown to be small protection indeed against a determined competitor, but rather by the ability of a company to attract and motivate the world's most talented engineers. We believe that applying the open source philosophy to our patents will strengthen rather than diminish Tesla's position in this regard.

Musk is clearly not afraid of competition. Instead, he embraces what it can bring not only to his company but to the entire world.

Competing Against Technology

Competition doesn't only come from organizations. It can come from technology. Just ask the music industry, whose history shows an unending trend of shifting to new and emerging media.

Inflation Adjusted 2013 Dollars (1973 to 2013)
US: $ In Millions; source: RIAA

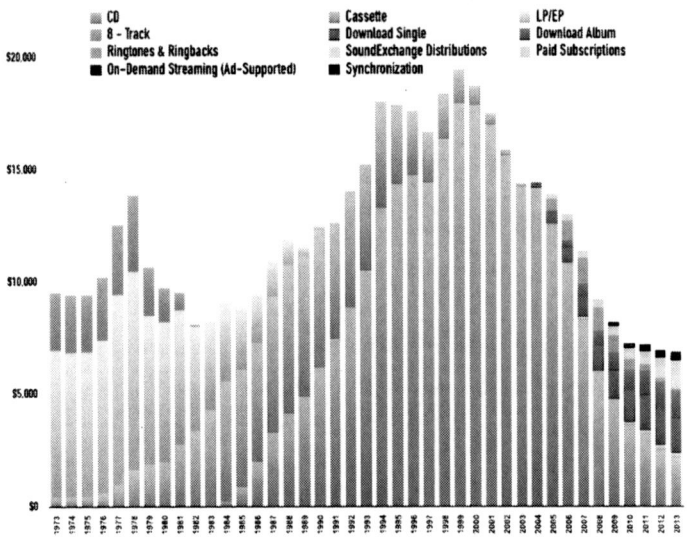

When file-sharing technology in the 90s enabled free downloading of music, the Recording Industry Association of America (RIAA) reacted with lawsuits and intimidation. Initially, they went after the file-sharing services themselves — most notably Napster — and generally won. Many of the services folded, and new services were prevented from springing up.

But, despite the legal success, file sharing still spread. Consumers continually found new technologies to perpetuate piracy.

So the RIAA went after the Internet service providers that hosted file-sharing servers. When that tactic failed, the RIAA went after the consumers themselves. During a period of nearly three years in the mid 2000s, the industry filed tens of thousands of lawsuits against individuals. By July 2006, the RIAA had brought lawsuits against more than 20,000 individuals in the United States to try to defend against file sharing.

At the same time, Apple cobbled together alliances with individual media companies. Capitalizing on the very technology the industry was battling, they developed their own media distribution methods to commercialize the practice and provide compensation to everyone in the creative value chain. The success of their response to new technology is clear.

Apple Still Underpins the Growth of the Digital Music Market

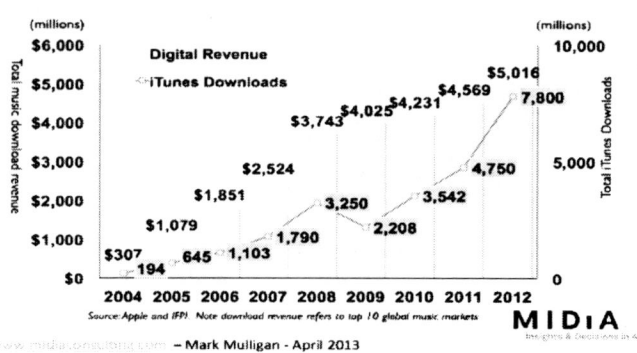

No matter how the RIAA had responded, the technological

change would have created a gut-wrenching period in their history. But imagine how much stronger the industry would be now had they embraced the new streaming technologies and carved out a leadership position rather than fighting it as a threat. Instead, they allowed Apple to carve that position out for itself — while making countless enemies through its scorched earth policy.

In Q1 2013, Apple made $2.4 billion from music — 63% of the digital music market — while Amazon made over $600 million and Google was growing its music download business aggressively. Meanwhile, consumers basically hate the recording industry. Even the artists it was supposedly protecting are increasingly seeking to fund themselves or go directly to the market without a label.

While it's easy to chide the RIAA in retrospect, it's also easy to see the difficulty in the never-ending nature of emerging technology. Today, Apple is struggling to avoid the same fate as the RIAA. Just as Apple's digital media ate into the physical media landscape ten years ago, today music streaming services like Pandora and Spotify are eating into Apple's revenue and engagement.

Apple is handling this type of technological competition in a few ways. For one, they've reacted by launched an audio streaming service of their own. For another, they've proactively sought out and bought the popular headphone line Beats by Dre. How their approaches to the latest technology pan out remains to be seen.

How Fear Sabotages Innovation

One of the best ways to fend off any threats is to innovate in a way that keeps you relevant with your customers and stays ahead of the competition. Innovation doesn't just have to be product innovation, but innovation can occur in process, customer service, and marketing.

The kind of innovation that spawns new product categories or business lines isn't for every company. Only a handful of truly great companies have the culture and capability to create this sort of competitive advantage. However, every company has the ability to differentiate and improve their product, service, or brand offerings in a way that takes control and ends the game of chasing the competition.

Innovation inherently takes an offensive posture, but fear can prevent even innovative approaches from being successful. The *Harvard Business Review* published an article entitled "11 Ways Big Companies Undermine Innovation." Among the eleven ways to undermine innovation, five were a result of, or rooted in, fear. One fairly high profile example of this comes from a company that many people might consider innovative — Facebook. However, beyond their flagship product, Facebook hasn't been able to create much new success.

Look at the graveyard of failed products or features introduced by Facebook: Poke, Gifts, Beacon, Graph Search, Camera, Facebook email, Places, and Deals. These were all hyped — by Facebook and others — as revolutionary new capabilities, products, and features with the possibility of being market disruptors. But when's the last time you've used one of them?

It's not that failing at product development is a sign of fear. Rather, it's how the company responds to those failures. According to a *Fast Company* article about Facebook's attempts to stay relevant for the second decade, their problem comes in getting these innovations off the ground. They lack patience and don't put in the work to adapt offerings and make them a success.

> Projects that did fight their way through the system faced other burdens rooted in the company's history. The "truth" of data is so paramount at Facebook that products were given little time to improve after launch. "A startup would try again or change it," that recently departed manager says of Facebook's graveyard of failed products. "But that kind of culture doesn't exist at Facebook. If something doesn't work off the bat, it's like, 'Okay, the metrics aren't working, let's put the engineers over here.' " One nasty by-product of this approach: demoralized employees.

Quitting too soon is as much a sign of fear as not trying new things at all. Both are fears of failure. Pulling the plug at the first sign of trouble is simply a later manifestation. Encountering the possibility of failure could just be a sign that a minor tweak is needed, but in a fear-driven company — especially one afraid of innovative competition — it's taken as the end.

Ed Catmull, the founder of Pixar, writes in *Creativity, Inc.* about the need for bravery in innovation:

> If you create a fearless culture, people will be much less hesitant to explore new areas, identifying

uncharted pathways and then charge down them. They will also begin to see the upside of decisiveness: the time they've saved by not gnashing their teeth about whether they're on the right course comes in handy when they hit a dead end and need to reboot.

It isn't enough to pick a path. You must go down it. By doing so, you see things you couldn't possibly see when you started out; you may not like what you see, some of it may be confusing, but at least you will have, as we like to say, "explored the neighborhood." The key point here is that even if you decide you're in the wrong place, there is still time to head toward the right place.

Scientists understand this. They know that "mistakes" lead to real discovery and breakthroughs. Despite being a proven model in science, it is almost never practiced in business because fear-dominated cultures see mistakes as the antithesis of a breakthrough, not its precursor.

The important element of innovation is being able to understand whether something needs to be tweaked or scrapped. Too many organizations see signs of trouble and make a knee-jerk, fear-based reaction rather than taking the time to assess all possible causes and potential ways to get the initiative on the right track. Fear of losing to the competition often clouds management's judgment — just when being able to remain focused bravely on the vision behind the initiative is so crucial for making a proper assessment of how to achieve success through innovation.

The Essex Revisited

At the center of the whaling industry, Nantucket's whaleships were all competing against each other. There were personal competitions among the captains and shareholders, fighting for the best men in town. At sea, they competed to get to the best fishing grounds.

The *Essex's* voyage was no different. The crew pushed their boat to gain whatever advantage they could. Philbrick gives an account in which the desire to pass other vessels led them to keep their sails high even in the face of an impending tropical storm. The aftermath speaks for itself:

> But the mood aboard the *Essex* sank into one of
> gloom. The ship had been severely damaged. Several
> sails, including both the main topgallant and the
> studding sail, had been torn into useless tatters. The
> cookhouse had been destroyed. The two whaleboats
> that had been hung off the port side of the ship
> had been torn from their davits and washed away,
> along with all their gear. The spare boat on the
> stern had been crushed by the waves. That left only
> two workable boats, and a whaleship required a
> minimum of three, plus two spares. Although the
> *Essex's* stern boat could be repaired, they would be
> without a single spare boat. Captain Pollard stared at
> the splintered mess and declared that they would be
> returning to Nantucket for repairs.
>
> His first mate, however, disagreed. Chase urged that
> they continue on, despite the damage. The chances
> were good, he insisted, that they would be able to

obtain spare whaleboats in the Azores, where they would soon be stopping to procure fresh provisions. Joy sided with his fellow mate. The captain's will was normally the law of the ship. But instead of ignoring his two younger mates, Pollard paused to consider their arguments. Four days into his first command, Captain Pollard reversed himself.

Compounded by the ship's politics (see Chapter 6), the fear of competition led to disastrous decisions.

A quick recap of the fear factors around competition:

1. **Self-knowledge**. Awareness of who and what your business is and how it best competes in the marketplace. And, perhaps most importantly, what your business is not.

2. **Leading vs. chasing**. How much your business chases the competition instead of focusing time and effort to grow your business in a way that makes sense for who you are.

3. **Technology**. The extent to which your market or industry is being disrupted either through technological change and innovation or through changes in consumer behavior.

4. **Innovation**. The role that innovation plays in your business and industry and how well your company executes on innovation.

8
FEAR INDICATOR
5 – REGULATION

"Government is part of business, any business."

— Phil Knight, Founder of Nike

W E OFTEN VIEW government regulatory bodies much like Tom sees Jerry during their scenes of literal cat and mouse. In some episodes, while Tom pursues Jerry with all the fervor of a competitor desperate for his next meal, his fervor often causes him to overlook the simple advantages he has over Jerry. This leads to Tom getting outsmarted into an empty outcome every time. Jerry, to add to Tom's frustration, often uses simple things to cast a more imposing image than his real-life stature.

This is how many managers and executives view regulators

— scared of a shadow that doesn't have the same ability to harm as the shadow might imply.

During a commencement address to Stanford University's business school in 2014, Nike founder Phil Knight spoke of the long and winding road his company took to become the international success it is today. One of the largest challenges Nike faced was a challenge from US Customs enforcing a little known part of code called the American Selling Price that dated to the 1930s. The enforcement action called for $25 million — at a time when Nike had annual sales of only $25 million.

Nike — which at the time had limited resources, no real political influence, and little experience with regulatory bodies — sprung into action. With the spunk of a small organization fighting for its life, they found ways to attack the problem instead of cowering like Tom from the shadow. They used the political establishments in the states where they had manufacturing and distribution facilities to lobby on their behalf, waged a PR campaign, and even knocked off their own product through a generic line to achieve the outcome they did. The process took nearly three years, but they found a way to settle for a much lower $9 million. At the same time, sales grew to over $400 million annually.

Perhaps most importantly, they didn't let the enforcement action take their focus away from serving their customers. They attacked the problem but didn't neglect the main advantage they were trying to protect — their market opportunity.

The Extent of Regulation

We call our elected representatives lawmakers. When problems manifest themselves, lawmakers hold hearings to determine the scope and size of the problem, what should be done about it, then potentially make a law to regulate it. Simple enough.

But a few lawmaking trends have contributed to an environment with an onslaught of regulatory problems for businesses.

1. A perception by many in American society that all problems must be addressed rather than chalking some unfortunate events up to just that — misfortune. We increasingly have a desire to prevent any little problem from ever occurring again. (This fear-based behavior is also discussed in Chapter 2.)

2. There is pressure to solve all problems through lawmaking. Even community issues that could be resolved at a community level are finding themselves bubbling up to higher levels of government. They're ultimately addressed with a broader set of solutions than necessary.

3. New regulatory agencies are created rather than adding some minor scope to existing organizations. This creates regulatory overlap and a complex web of sometimes conflicting goals and rules.

This general trend is depicted in the following graph that shows regulatory activity during the two-year period following the Great Recession. Note that the amount of regulation coming from America and global regulations dwarfs that of Europe and Asia.

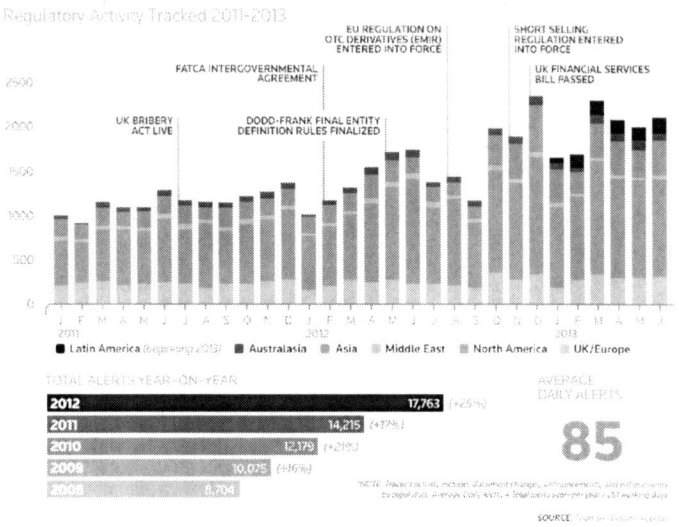

And as you might expect, CEOs' attitudes toward this amount of regulation has continued to show increasing amounts of strain.

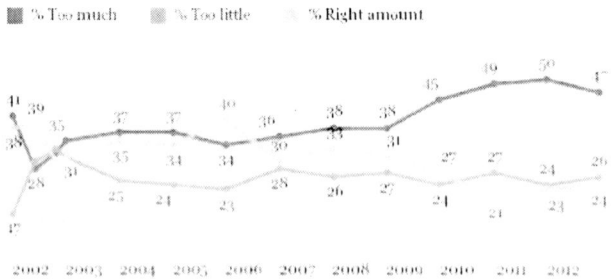

However, that is purely for context. I'm focusing on the impact of these regulations rather than reducing regulations. Plenty of organizations are tackling the growing regulatory context. There's Small Businesses for Sensible Regulations, an initiative launched in 2011 by the National Federation of Independent Business. The US Chamber of Commerce started its own Project on Regulatory Reform that same year. And George Mason University's Mercatus Center runs a Regulatory Studies Program that not only analyzes the regulatory process, but also explores market-based alternatives that achieve the same goals as regulations. Small business even has their own regulatory watchdog inside the federal government: the Small Business Administration's Office of Advocacy, which tries to make sure that agencies consider the impact of their rules on small firms.

Industry-Specific Regulation

From 1997 to 2010, only four industries saw a reduction in regulation — Crop Production, Data Processing/Hosting, Real Estate, and Machinery Manufacturing. Despite increases in regulatory activity by most industries, the majority of regulation is aimed at a handful of industries. These include Healthcare and Financial Services.

The mindset that regulation creates can even be detrimental to individual success. For a time in 2013, I flirted with the idea of taking a Vice President position at Macy's. Early in my discussions with their executive recruiter, I was told that my candidacy could be hurt by the fact that the majority of my career had been spent in heavily regulated businesses. It was their experience that people with experience in those industries viewed things as too black or white.

The last and possibly biggest side effect is the increasing amount of personnel needed to handle this increasing load of regulations. Compliance officer employment in the finance and insurance industry is projected to rise 11.1% nationwide from 2012 to 2022. That's more than double the 4.8% growth projected for other banking jobs during the same period.

This trend has had an especially profound impact on higher education. A significant proportion of tuition increases has come from hiring administrators. Since 2001, the number of college administrators has increased 50% faster than the number of instructors, according to the Education Department. Some cases are stunning, like the University of Minnesota, which added 1,000 administrators in the past decade, reaching a ratio of one administrator for every 3.5 students. Arizona State University increased the number of administrators by 94% between 1993 and 2007, according to the Goldwater Institute, and the University of Pennsylvania non-teaching staff swelled by 83%.

While administrative jobs may not sound like compliance, a 2014 *Huffington Post* article provides a finer point:

> There are thousands of regulations governing the distribution of financial aid alone. And probably every college or university that's accredited, they've got at least one person with a major portion of their time dedicated to that, and in some cases whole office staffs. These aren't bad things to do, but somebody's got to do them. Since 1987, universities have also started or expanded departments devoted to

marketing, diversity, disability, sustainability, security, environmental health.

Inside some organizations, there are now as many people checking the work as there making business decisions. With an ever-increasing amount of people peering over shoulders of line personnel and managers, the seeds of mistrust continue to grow.

As has been previously stated, confusion is a key source or amplifying factor for fear. Regulation is no different. Not only do many regulations run counter to reasonable business practices, but there is often confusion amidst the lawmakers' original law, the regulatory agencies rules, the interpretation of the guidance, and the implications of non-compliance.

To depict this confusion, JP Morgan Chase put together a diagram of the landscape.

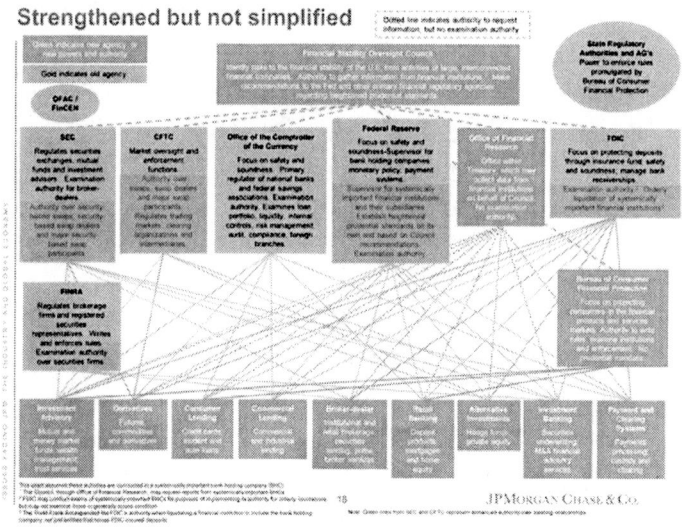

Totally clear, right? No area of the bank interacts with

fewer than four agencies. With so much overlap between regulatory bodies, it is easy to see how confusion could reign.

This confusion doesn't happen only with bureaucratic governmental agencies. It can also occur with standards organizations providing quasi-oversight and best practice recommendations. A *Bloomberg Business* article on the international shipping company Maersk details a dispute over what sort of glass to install along the bridge wings that dragged on for two weeks between it and its partner Daewoo Shipbuilding:

> Unlike on most container ships, where the walkways on either side of the pilothouse are open to the elements, the Triple-E's were to be enclosed. Pointing out that international standards required a "clear view" from the bridge, Maersk insisted that the glass in those wing windows be heated, with windshield wipers, as it was for the pilothouse. But DSME argued that heated glass and wipers, while clearly required for the pilothouse, were unnecessary on the bridge wings, and that "clear view" simply meant "window." At stake was $100,000 in costs.
>
> The companies appealed to the American Bureau of Shipping, an international classification society, which was unable to resolve the dispute. Eventually they reached a compromise: a mix of heated and unheated panes on each bridge wing; some with wipers.

Confusion can even happen from rumored regulation and events that are seen as triggers for regulatory review.

I once ran an operations center in the banking industry,

specifically mortgage banking. We served in a compliance function on behalf of the banks. Each morning, I read news blasts from the industry to identify anything that might have caused panic. If an item happened to slip through our review, we would receive panicked calls from mortgage-servicing managers mid-morning, desperate for an answer about some obscure operational detail.

We often sent proactive communications simply to avoid the appearance that we were not on top of the situation. It took hard work to keep their fear from infecting our culture.

Advisors Creating Fear

With a proliferation of regulations, sometimes a company needs a whole other company to help sort through it — often with problematic results. A 2013 *Time* magazine article chronicles the story of a little-known business named Promontory that was wielding an outsize influence on the financial regulatory environment.

To enforce the escalating regulations coming out of the financial crisis of 2008, regulators were using firms like Promontory. At the same time, firms like Promontory were selling services to achieve compliance to the very businesses they were regulating, an obvious conflict of interest. The article elaborates:

> By the time he left government in 1998, Ludwig realized that the growing size and complexity of financial institutions would lead to ever more labyrinthine regulation. Federal officials found it as

difficult to enforce rules as banks did to comply with them. Promontory stepped into the breach, advising both sides. In recent years, Promontory reportedly charged up to $1,500 / hour for its services. [These] private regulators not only police bank practices; they are often tasked with forcing banks to mend their ways. [The practice is so widespread that] even private regulators find themselves stretched to capacity and have outsourced the work to still other contractors.

At the insurance company I worked for, we had a long-simmering compliance issue that was being addressed in a multi-year plan. However, some executives became concerned that we had not reported the issue properly.

While self-reporting is a good idea in theory, it can be problematic if you haven't quantified the issue and have no timeline for compliance — which was exactly our situation. In order to help, the team brought in a Big Four accounting firm with experience in insurance regulation. Not only would they help us craft a plan, they would also go on our behalf to the insurance commissioner as independent oversight and provide the people (entry-level accountants) to help us do the remediation and restitution work. Problem solved?

As of this writing, more than a year after my departure and a full two years after being engaged, the accounting firm is still on-site. At various points during the process, the team swelled to over 50 people with monthly billings nearing $1 million.

This, in itself, is a problem. But, as with Promontory, it goes deeper. When meeting with the regulators, sometimes the only people in the room were a partner at the firm, a former insurance commissioner, and an outside attorney — all people with incentive to continue the process rather than resolve it.

It wasn't the first time this particular accounting firm had operated in this way. During their pitch to senior management, they even extolled the virtues of the fact that they had been engaged in hundreds of such regulatory cases. The same message was offered from the other two Big Four accounting firms that were interviewed.

Which makes a sane businessperson wonder the same thing that Ohio Senator Sherrod Brown did when interviewing an OCC official during public hearings: "If a consulting firm... has repeatedly been, for lack of a better term, at the scene of the crime, what would it take before they are viewed as not qualified?'"

Senator Brown went on to develop legislation with other lawmakers to give regulators authority to punish consultants using powers similar to those they can use against the very financial services firms they are being hired to help regulate. Which almost works out to be anti-regulation regulation.

The *Time* article has this final shot at these firms:

> But the bank is paying the monitor, the monitor
> is living at the bank, coziness develops, and if you
> don't have a regulator checking in to say, "What have
> you found? Where are you looking?" it's a recipe
> for disaster.

It's easy to see how these types of arrangements sow fear. With such vast financial benefit in producing a steady stream of bad news, no wonder firms have cozied up to the executives in charge, thrown the company's people under the bus, and mischaracterized the level of risk — all in the name of regulatory compliance.

But in most cases — including at my former company — senior executives have no way to reverse course. Given the non-compliance, they're not in a position to march into the regulator's office, since they need the insurance commissioner to believe the project was under control.

Stepping back from the quandary, what could have prevented the whole mess? Perhaps allowing the team to continue along the path they were on rather than reacting with fear. The issue would have been quantified, and a clear timeline for restitution would have been presented within a matter of months. That information would have allowed the general counsel to report to the insurance commissioner, and we could have had the plan approved by the regulator at that time.

But the fear of headlines and possibility of what a regulator might do forced management to rush to action. Two years and millions of dollars later, the organization was not much closer to remediation.

Opportunity in Regulation

At the beginning of this chapter, I presented a lot of data as the backdrop to growing levels of regulatory fear. However, I contend that it is less about the amount of regulation that creates this fear and more about the state of mind of the organization regarding regulation and compliance.

Does your organization take the literal view of compliance? Or do you try to understand what is driving the regulation in an attempt to find new novel approaches to address the issue that regulation is attempting to control?

At the insurance company, I joined a division that sold lender-placed insurance to banks, mortgage lenders, and financial institutions in 2007. Lender-placed insurance was a fairly obscure insurance product that became more broadly known after the mortgage crisis. The insurance policy was to insure mortgage property in which lenders had a financial interest but was uninsured by borrowers.

The product got swept up into the mortgage reform effort and came under attack because of abuses by some lenders and insurers charging exorbitant rates. Using the fees as a new revenue stream, abusive agents and lenders would falsely place this insurance on borrowers who in fact had voluntary policies. This drove some borrowers — already on the brink of foreclosure — closer to the edge of the cliff.

As a result of the mortgage reform efforts — and because of escalating costs being passed on to it by lenders — Fannie Mae became interested in the marketplace in late 2011. In February 2012, we received a request from Fannie Mae to meet at their offices to discuss the lender-placed marketplace and work together to improve it. While the objective sounded very altruistic, make no mistake about their motivations. Fannie Mae was first and foremost interested in driving their own costs down and scoring political points on behalf of trampled-on borrowers.

As you can imagine, the call from Fannie Mae created a lot of executive hand-wringing. They felt as though margins and growth potential would be threatened by cooperating with Fannie Mae, but they also felt it presented an opportunity.

Fannie Mae executives made no bones about the fact that they felt another company was responsible for the current market issues, giving us an even greater opportunity to make some serious waves.

Our executives were very reluctant to upset our agents — our primary distribution channel — by working with Fannie Mae and putting the agents' margins at risk. However, over the previous few years, there had already been enough margin contraction and focus on scale that momentum was driving toward a few very large general agents that would continue to drive margin contraction. We had good relationships with these agents, and cooperating with Fannie Mae could have worked in our favor by positioning it as though we were protecting their access to the market.

I made the argument that we should go all in with Fannie Mae. It would be a cut in profit margin, but it would mean a dramatically larger revenue base and greater long-term prospects. We could continue to battle for smaller accounts and eventually work our way up to 15% market share, or we could take a bold risk and partner with Fannie Mae and their new government overseers the Federal Housing Finance Association to become a dominant leader in the market. Clearly the strategy had significant risk, but the market was evolving rapidly. Plus, it would have been good public relations and might have dramatically reshaped the industry.

Leading up to the meeting, we struggled to gain consensus on our approach. There was still reluctance to show any of our cards to Fannie Mae. Being anchored to our legacy distribution channel, the most senior executives had a clear fear of losing what we had. This kept us from getting out in front of Fannie Mae and leading the industry.

What resulted was a shaky commitment from us to the Fannie Mae executives — a weird form of fence-sitting that they saw right through. Toward the end of the meeting, our EVP was challenged directly on our willingness to leave our old distribution model.

The process played out over the next several months. While we put together a strong proposal — so strong that the industry began to believe that we were the frontrunners — the lack of perceived commitment doomed our bid. Fannie Mae ultimately decided to do nothing.

Ultimately, our fear of going all in and abandoning a failing business model prevented us — and the industry — from making a big splash. A missed opportunity.

And that's the real lesson here. Not just that fear can cause missed opportunities. But that regulation can create opportunities — if you're willing to act bravely.

A successful case is the CVS drugstore chain. In 2014, CVS made a public relations splash by discontinuing the sale of cigarettes. This was no isolated decision. Rather, it was part of a bigger transformation that CVS has undergone to take full advantage of the Affordable Care Act. The *New Yorker* describes the transformation:

> More than fifty years after CVS was founded, the company is overhauling its identity. As of Wednesday, CVS has renamed itself CVS Health and, as part of its rebranding, the company will no longer sell tobacco products. (The *Times* published a photograph

taken inside one CVS, in Manhattan, where a cigarette display had been replaced by anti-smoking signs. One of them reads, "We quit tobacco. Ask a trained pharmacist or nurse practitioner to help you quit, too.") The company's logo now includes a friendly-looking red heart; its Web site proclaims, "Our name has changed, but our purpose remains the same: helping people on their path to better health."

What inspired CVS's rhetorical shift from saving pennies to saving lives? Again, as in the sixties, a change in the law has presented businesses with an opportunity. The Affordable Care Act of 2010, which expanded Medicaid coverage and required more people to buy health insurance, has helped push down the percentage of uninsured people in the US. Not only does it hope to fill more prescriptions for newly insured people, but it also wants to provide people with reimbursable health-care services, like what they might get at a doctor's office.

Today, CVS operates about nine hundred "Minute Clinics" in its stores, where nurse practitioners and physician assistants treat and write prescriptions for ailments like strep throat, bladder infections, and joint sprains; they can also provide physicals to kids entering college and perform lab tests for people with conditions like diabetes or high blood pressure. CVS hopes to operate fifteen hundred of these clinics by 2017. On top of that, CVS runs a huge and growing business, known as CVS/Caremark, which operates prescription-drug programs for companies and insurers and negotiates prices for pharmacies.

Brave organizations take a proactive approach to regulation — not for ensuring compliance but for shaping the regulation and leading the way for other industry players. This requires a significant investment in the political process and building relationships with regulators. This relationship-building can't happen if the starting perspective from senior managers and executives is that of regulators as adversaries. It also requires visionary leaders who anticipate shifting consumer attitudes. This enables a business to take the high ground rather than protecting business models that will eventually fail.

The Effect of Centralized Compliance

As we've seen, businesses are affected by fears from a dizzying amount of regulation, by advisors who are financially motivated to perpetuate these fears, and by an inability to see regulation as an opportunity.

As one last wrinkle, corporations themselves compound regulatory fears by centralizing their compliance functions and abdicating responsibility to bureaucratic compliance officers.

You have likely seen or heard statements from them, like, "Compliance is everyone's responsibility." Supposedly engaging the business toward cooperation, these compliance teams don't truly mean what they say. They believe in a broken model that puts a central team in charge of understanding and interpreting regulation while putting the business teams at arm's length distance from the very thing they are best suited to control.

The results are dictates based on the compliance team's interpretation of the regulations — yet another regulatory layer. These teams can wind up operating much like the aforementioned accounting firms — often out of self-preservation — by lording regulatory information over others in the organization, working to get the resources and outcomes they want. (See Chapter 6 for more on politics and resource allocation.)

Since many compliance teams are the only interface to executives, they can operate like this freely. They're considered the authority rather than the business practitioners who see the ultimate impacts on consumer behavior, pricing, and sales. Following their lead can easily have a negative impact on business goals — or, worse, core values.

We put so much energy into regulations but so little effort into investigating, indicating, and integrating core values. Enforcement is more convenient for a fearful organization.

It takes less courage to write rules and hand out punishments than it does to provide a vision and reinforce core beliefs. But bravely providing vision and reinforcing core beliefs are the way to turning regulation away from being a fear factor and into becoming an opportunity.

The conflict between ownership and stewardship tends to influence outcomes regarding the effectiveness of compliance groups and limiting the impact of sowing the seeds of fear in an organizational context.

Ownership leads to centralized teams that are disconnected from the impact of day to day business decisions. These centralized compliance groups are oftentimes funded by under-resourcing the very teams that are most able to provide stewardship over the long-term health of the business.

An attitude of stewardship would resource the business teams appropriately and provide the authority to ensure compliance. This would be done by embedding compliance as a responsibility instead of pulling it out into a separate organization, creating bureaucratic overhead and the opportunity for politics and mistrust to interfere.

Detractors of this approach will be quick to yell about the need for independence to avoid being pulled into competing business priorities. However, that doesn't become a problem if managers are resourced appropriately and held accountable for their effectiveness. Additionally, any trade-off of independence is more than made up by having personnel that better understand the complexities of compliance within the context of day to day decision making.

A quick recap of the fear factors around regulation:

1. **The extent of regulation.** Particularly related to your industry.

2. **Advisors.** How much of a voice and authority does your organization allow consultants and compliance analysts to have in day-to-day matters? Advisors can play a key role in perpetuating compliance fear, often at the cost of your team's morale.

3. **Opportunity.** Is the company taking the lead and creating a competitive advantage from the emerging regulations or are they just trying to protect their core businesses? Fear can lead to pretending that the

regulation will have minimal impact on long-term business prospects.

4. **Centralized compliance**. A heavy centralized focus on regulation can increase fear, as can the level of redundancy between regulatory groups; audit, risk management and compliance.

9

FEAR INDICATOR 6 – RISK AND CONTROL

"A lot of people think if you just had more process and more compliance — checks and double-checks and so forth — you could create a better result in the world. Well, Berkshire has had practically no process. We had hardly any Internal Auditing until they forced it on us. We just try to operate in a seamless web of deserved trust and be careful whom we trust."

— Charlie Munger, Berkshire Hathaway

LET ME START by saying that, as I began writing this chapter, I knew it would likely generate the most blow-back of any in the book. Partly because I have a lot of friends and former colleagues in this industry, but also because it is such a sacred cow. I will likely hear from chief audit officers, chief risk officers, investor advocates, and corporate governance professionals about how I am dead wrong on this subject. After all, how can you argue against control? It's akin to arguing against police or fire departments.

But I think we blindly — and mistakenly — throw increasing amounts of money at the issue and never ask for accountability or ask questions about the effectiveness of our approaches and investments.

Risk Assessment is Broken

Even the most ardent risk and control zealots will have to admit that many risk and control structures and processes are broken. If they weren't broken, we wouldn't continue to have massive headline-inducing corporate governance breakdowns such as Enron, Tyco, and Lehman Brothers. Despite the Sarbanes-Oxley Act and much more aggressive regulatory agencies such as the Securities and Exchange Commission, job losses due to failing companies continue to rise.

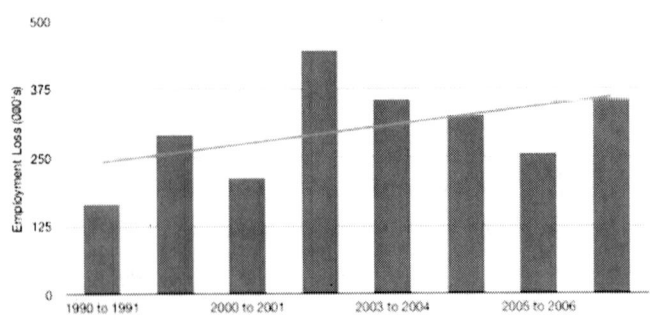

Source - US Census Bureau, 2012 Statistical Abstract

Yes, one could argue that the increasing job losses are the result of unprecedented technological change disrupting industries and leaving companies that don't adapt in the dust. However, technological change is a constant, and corporate governance has a role in staying in front of technological change as well. All good risk assessments must include the risk of disruption along with corporate fraud. So there must be an evaluation of our corporate governance and risk assessment approaches when considering our general inability to stem the tide of large corporate failures.

By way of background for those unfamiliar with the risk management process, it is common to evaluate risk on a two-by-two grid charting impact and likelihood.

Impact	High /Low	High /High
	Low /Low	Low /High
	Likelihood	

The quadrant where impact and likelihood are both high is typically where risk managers focus their efforts — adding controls and spending resources to guard against or recover from risk.

How these are assessed depends on the organization. The assessment is a fine line between being a responsible organization that wants to protect itself against a failure and a company that is being guided by fear. As an example, the risk of fraud is often labeled as a high likelihood. Yet according to the annual report from Kroll, a global risk management consulting firm, the incidence of most types of fraud was under 20%, with many in the single digits and none greater than 28%. Furthermore, when fraud did occur, 32% of the events were perpetrated by a senior or middle manager — the very people who provide input into the risk assessment process, not the entry-level people the controls are typically aimed at.

Additionally, risk factors vary widely based on industry and geographic region:

> Globalization has changed the way business operates. Companies have for some years now been in search of bigger international markets, while at the same time striving to become leaner. Less appreciated is that these shifts, however profitable, lead to a higher risk of fraud in a variety of ways. For example, 30% of respondents report that entering new, riskier markets has increased their exposure to fraud in the past year. The United States has an incidence of fraud below the overall average — 66% of companies were hit by one fraud in the last year compared to 70% globally — and a rate of loss that is also slightly under the norm — 1.2% compared to 1.4% for the survey as a whole.

Despite the data, risk managers typically assess based on headlines, not actual probabilities. This gap in perception and reality is shown in the following chart from the Kroll report showing how some industries spend an inordinate amount of resources relative to the amount of industry-specific fraud damage.

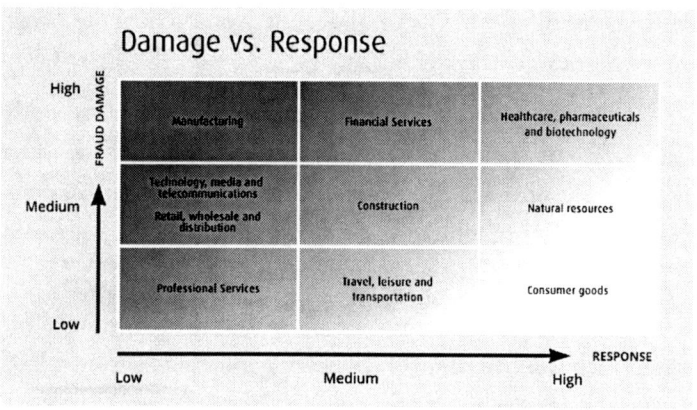

I equate it to how much insurance we buy as individuals. On average, 83% of households buy homeowners insurance, 86% of drivers buy auto insurance, 41% buy life insurance and 49% buy short-term disability. It is reasonable, even mandated in some cases, to buy insurance. But the decision isn't as simple as responsible or not. At the end of the day, the decision is ultimately about the probability of something bad happening and the least costly way to recover from it.

Is it irresponsible for a single person with limited assets to not buy life insurance? No. If anything, it might be irresponsible and wasteful to buy it, considering a healthy, young person's circumstances. But, in the current fear-based environment of absolute governance truths, that practicality is often missing.

Even the process of risk management begins with fear in the form of a risk assessment. It often consists of a handful of managers, auditors, risk managers, and business owners sitting in a room and listing all the things that could go wrong with a business. This risk assessment process causes a focus on the big, headline-worthy things while overlooking the small things that can create the big things.

To use an individual example again, look again at the odds of dying chart from Chapter 2. It clearly shows that the most likely causes of death are heart disease or cancer. Yet we continue to overeat or smoke while worrying about the headlines of airplane crashes and terrorist attacks.

This same phenomenon occurs in business. We focus on business continuity, disaster recovery, fraud, and lawsuits when the real issues are bad managers, lack of cooperation between divisions, and lack of vision by senior management. I'm not saying that risk assessment is bad. I'm saying that, in its usual form, it isn't really effective at assessing risk.

The Only Voice

Mark Andreesen, the founder of Netscape and now billionaire venture capitalist — says this about the impact of the Sarbanes-Oxley Act on liquidity for new ventures through initial public offerings: "It's this idea that if you control everything down to the nth detail, nothing will go wrong. It's this bizarre, bureaucratic, top-down mentality that if only we could make everything predictable, then everything would be magic, everything would be wonderful."

What Andreesen is speaking of is a nasty by-product in which, instead of being a voice of reason helping an organization come to a balanced decision, risk management is the lone voice, constantly shouting for risk aversion and even fear.

Chronicling the rising influence of chief risk officers in

the banking industry, a *Wall Street Journal* article describes how decision-making now occurs within the executive ranks at Wells Fargo:

> "Five years ago, if the risk group recommended against a strategy or product, it might just be one part of a debate," he says. Now, "when we say no, it's usually no."

> Mr. Loughlin is an example of the naysayers who are gaining power and multiplying in number across the US banking industry as financial institutions bend to pressure from regulators to make their operations safer and simpler following the financial crisis that began in 2008.

With each corporate crisis, legislation and regulation put more and more emphasis on risk and control as the solution. The end result is reams of great-looking heatmaps, process flows, and neatly documented controls, but no real results.

Corporate America has lost the forest for the trees. The same risk managers and auditors who are responsible for documenting these assessments are either too junior to truly understand the risk dynamics or not skilled enough to work with management to make the business-appropriate changes best able to prevent failure from occurring.

At the age of 26, I had my first opportunity to not only sit in on, but also participate in the agenda for board meetings of a publicly traded company. With a role on the audit committee, I saw first-hand how accountability worked between shareholders and management in a Board of Directors — and how it didn't work.

A fellow member of the audit committee was Bo Schembechler, the former football coach of the Michigan Wolverines. While it was an honor to meet and work with Coach Schembechler, I must admit I was surprised that he was on the committee. He had tremendous leadership experience from his decades of coaching, but I wondered what qualified him to audit. As each successive quarter passed, the only audit-related contributions I saw him make were complaints about the volume of documentation requiring his reading and analysis. Later, I learned he was a close family friend of the CEO.

Don't get me wrong. His leadership experience was tremendously valuable to the executive management team. But his contributions on the audit committee were minimal at best. I say this to underscore the fact that much "governance" is window dressing. Yet it has tremendous implications on the level of fear throughout the organization and on the amount of business bravery that can be generated for crucial business decisions.

Studies of the effectiveness of internal control systems are rare, but some are dispelling the idea that more equals better, such as the research of professors Margit Osterloh and Bruno S. Frey at the University of Zurich:

> Strict control has a paradoxical effect. It leads to a never-ending and continuously expanding need to increase control. In view of the intensive interdependencies that characterize firms, this is a futile endeavor. Moreover, such an exercise seriously affects the loyalty of employees to their firms. In laboratory experiments, it was shown that negative sanctions crowd out intrinsically motivated trust (Bohnet, Frey & Huck 2001; see Fehr & List 2002,

who find similar results). Low levels of legal contract enforcement crowd in trustworthiness. Thus, more order results from less law.

That is a very non-traditional view of internal control and risk management. But it's a well-founded thought that should be explored. I keep expecting to reach the point where boards and management start demanding a better return on all this risk management spending. Yet I see no one interested in being brave enough to challenge the status quo and offer real, compelling solutions.

And there are plenty already in action. Berkshire Hathaway — which has no General Counsel or Human Resources department — believes the best way to overcome this typical alignment of interests is through a fairly simple accountability model:

> The best way to hold managers accountable is to make them eat their own cooking. [Warren Buffett's right-hand man Charlie] Munger pointed to the late Columbia University philosophy professor, Charles Frankel, who believed "that systems are responsible in proportion to the degree in which the people making the decisions are living with the results of those decisions."

Ed Catmull at Pixar has a similar mentality: "If all our careful planning cannot prevent problems, then our best method of response is to enable employees at every level to own the problems and have the confidence to fix them."

The problem is that many companies' leadership has no reason to change. Boards and management can hide behind the perception of control. They use the additional investment in control and corporate governance to prove they are committed to best practices while operating for their own, short-term self-interests — the very motivations that demanded internal control in the first place.

Imbalanced Risk Management

While risk management can include corporate governance systems, risk management groups and compliance, one component tends to generate an outsize case of organizational fear: the Internal Audit function.

Criticizing Internal Audit is hardly earthshaking. In January 2012, Ernst & Young commissioned Forbes Insights to conduct a global survey about the evolving role of Internal Audit. Respondents included audit executives, C-suite executives, and board members representing organizations with global revenues of $500 million or more and spanning 26 industry sectors. The findings weren't exactly positive:

- On the question of "What sort of impact has strong organizational risk management had on your long-term earnings performance?" 20% said it was somewhat or strongly negative.

- On the question of "How would you rate your organization's Internal Audit function today?" 41% indicated it was not effective in varying degrees.

- Lastly, for the question "Does Internal Audit have an explicit and documented mandate aligned to business?" 52% said, "No, independent from the overarching business strategy."

- So what is it about audit that seems to generate more fear than results?

Audit, risk management, and compliance groups are full of people who have a very black and white view of the world. I know. I spent the first ten years of my career in audit. During that time, personality assessments overwhelmingly rated my colleagues as SJs in the Myers-Briggs Type Indicator parlance:

> SJs are observant, stable and motivated by a need to maintain security. They are realistic, routinized administrators requiring tasks be completed correctly and that people behave appropriately. SJs make thorough examinations to ensure everything is done according to plan. They make sure no more and no less credit is given than due. When a need arises, they are quick to provide a solution, provided that the need is justified. SJs are not driven by impulse, but rather by concrete fact.

In other words, they look for the most literal interpretations. That works great for combing through thousands of claim files or payables transactions — both very necessary. However, audit teams also need to work with businesspeople and interpret business situations that are full of grays.

Audit tools themselves are black and white, forcing people into formulaic thinking and allowing real risks to be missed. In my experience, including with Big Four auditing firms, training starts with template work plans like checklists. While they are a great way to make entry-level auditors productive quickly, they establish a reliance on a yes or no approach rather than developing critical thinking. When it comes to deciding why certain controls are good for certain types of risks, audit teams lack both tools and preparation.

But the desire for better methods exists. In the sixteen years I have been around audit groups, everyone says they would like to implement continuous auditing approaches — a philosophy that builds in automatic controls and early warning signs. An example would be a data warehouse system that reports any payments with same payee, amount, and date as a duplicate payment. Compared to pulling a sample of 500 every few years and examining it, continuous auditing provides better coverage, saves time, and is more effective. No wonder everyone wants to implement it.

Yet very few audit groups make the transition. For one, it's easy to fall back on older tools. For another, many older, ineffective approaches are endorsed by regulatory agencies. Though everyone has realized that a risk-based approach provides better coverage, the Sarbanes-Oxley Act mandates an approach similar to the old models. So the effort to create more effective approaches can actually be penalized.

What results from rigid thinkers using broken tools and approaches? Rory Sutherland's TED Talk gives a picture:

> So people who believed in psychological solutions didn't have a model. We didn't have a framework. This is what Warren Buffett's business partner Charlie Munger calls "a latticework on which to hang your ideas." Engineers, economists, classical economists all had a very, very robust existing latticework on which practically every idea could be hung. We merely have a collection of

random individual insights without an overall model. And what that means is that in looking at solutions, we've probably given too much priority to what I call technical engineering solutions, Newtonian solutions, and not nearly enough to the psychological ones.

Why were we not given the chance to solve this problem psychologically? I think it's because there's an imbalance, an asymmetry, in the way we treat creative, emotionally-driven psychological ideas versus the way we treat rational, numerical, spreadsheet-driven ideas. If you're a creative person, I think quite rightly, you have to share all your ideas for approval with people much more rational than you. You have to go in and you have to have a cost-benefit analysis, a feasibility study, an ROI study and so forth. And I think that's probably right. But this does not apply the other way around. People who have an existing framework, an economic framework, an engineering framework, feel that actually logic is its own answer. What they don't say is, "Well the numbers all seem to add up, but before I present this idea, I'll go and show it to some really crazy people to see if they can come up with something better." And so we, artificially I think, prioritize what I'd call mechanistic ideas over psychological ideas.

Again, it's too much black and white. What it ultimately leads to is making the perfect the enemy of the good. In order to separate themselves from their peers, to feel good about their work, and to go above and beyond, audit teams target things that are not perfect, even if they're largely good.

With their mindset and tools, they're all but required to find something. An audit or report with no exceptions could be seen as a sign of failure. There's an implicit fear of reporting nothing in case something gets identified at a later date, implying that the audit or risk management team was asleep at the wheel.

How to avoid this? As a first step, hire good businesspeople. Then, look for — and possibly even train — good audit and risk management skills. During my three years in Internal Audit, I often thought I would be a much better auditor after having spent time in the business. So, I moved into a line of business. After a few years of that, I spoke with people in Internal Audit about opportunities. A consistent theme was their concern about my having been out of audit for five years.

That attitude was really a symptom of a systematic bias within Internal Audit. Many audit teams are stacked with former public accounting employees who have never had to be accountable for decisions. They sit on the sidelines as armchair quarterbacks, steering business decisions without ever having been responsible for business decisions.

While there is no reliable data on the number of auditors with prior line of business positions, my experience suggests it's a very low percentage. The typical career progression is to start in public accounting, move to an Internal Audit group, then eventually move into a financial or technical position. Rarely does that career progression happen in the opposite direction. And if a career progression does happen in that reverse order, it typically indicates something less than successful.

The people and tools of Internal Audit aren't just naturally black and white — they seem to be stuck that way.

The Broken Model

The net effect of all the inertia around risk and control is that management does its own thing. They use assessments to punish the process owners, to make political points for greater organizational control, or to further their own pet projects. Business owners see this and disregard what the assessments say about their actual work.

This creates a cycle. As management uses risk and audit teams, the risk and audit teams gain power organizationally. Process owners who disregard the assessments score successively worse. Their declining scores justify the need for larger audit teams. And so on. Not coincidentally, it looks similar to the fear cycle introduced in Chapter 3.

Despite how the Great Recession doubled the unemployment rate from 4.6% to 9.6%, very few companies ever decreased their budget for Internal Audit, and the auditor profession grew by 13% during this period.

A similar trend played out for risk management and compliance groups across corporate America. According to a 2014 *Wall Street Journal* report, Wells Fargo had 2,300 employees in its core risk-management department, up from 1,700 two years prior, and the department's annual budget had doubled to $500 million in the same period. The company's overall workforce had remained flat.

To put that in perspective, Wells Fargo's Risk Management department was larger than all but 0.09% of American businesses.

Complexity in Structures and Roles

Adding to the fear dynamic, the various groups and departments involved in corporate governance often lack role definition — even while structures get more and more complex, as demonstrated by this chart of a typical corporate governance structure.

Somehow, there is both overlap among roles and holes in coverage. Confusion is the friend of fear, and the more confusion that exists, the more fertile the ground for fear to develop and grow. When it comes to corporate governance, that fear most obviously contributes to the bloat seen in the Wells Fargo statistics, but it even leads to uncertainty about risk itself.

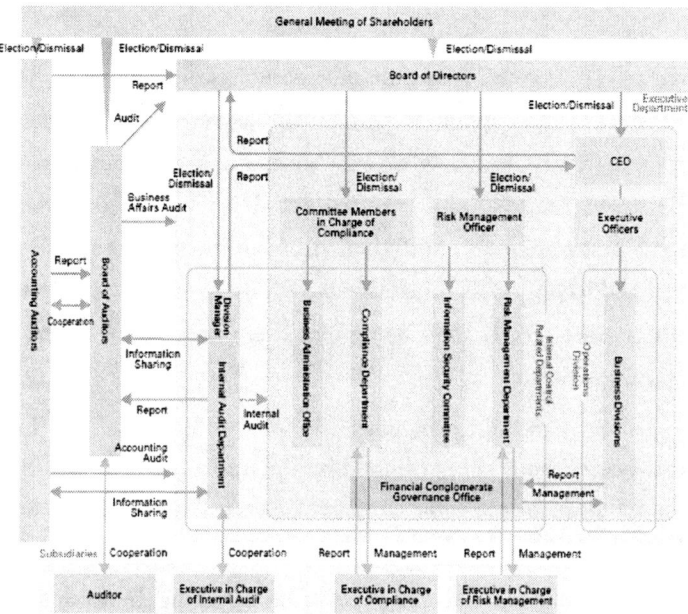

As a former risk management practitioner, I always saw confusion about how audit was different from risk management. Often, after an audit was performed on an area, the risk management team soon did an assessment of the same area. As you can imagine, many of the same questions would be asked, and a lot of the same testing would occur.

More importantly, to the business group it felt inefficient, redundant, and as if they were being targeted. It's easy to imagine how this fear affected their decisions and prevented bravery. I might even be willing to argue that fear is a greater harm than almost any risk trying to be prevented or managed. But I think I've already invited enough blowback.

The Essex Revisited

We talked earlier in this chapter about assessment bias. The decision-making made at seas by the leadership of the *Essex* is the ultimate example of how assessment bias can lead to disastrous results. While Pollard and Nickerson didn't create a risk assessment to guide their decision-making, they clearly weighed the impact and likelihood of cannibals in Tahiti much more greatly than being lost at sea and their own eventual cannibalism.

Their inability to calculate true probability of getting lost at sea came from being blinded by the unrealistic probabilities chattered up in the echo chamber of their Nantucket culture. According to the book, this culture blinded them:

Nantucketers were suspicious of anything beyond their immediate experience. Their far-reaching success in whaling was founded not on radical technological advances or bold gambles but on a profound conservatism. Gradually building on the achievements of the generations before them, they had expanded their whaling empire in a most deliberate and painstaking manner. If new information didn't come to them from the lips of another Nantucketer, it was suspect.

Every industry and company is susceptible of this same assessment bias leading to poor decision-making.

A quick recap of the fear factors around risk and control:

1. **Broken assessments**. Because of estimation bias, the process of risk assessment through heat maps and the

like often ignores whole risk universes and provides incomplete or misdirected guidance.

2. **The only voice.** Corporate governance has often gone from being one voice among many to being the biggest voice or the only voice.

3. **Imbalance.** The people and tools of risk management lack balance. Instead of understanding how certain business situations affect decision-making, risk management operates on too-literal principles.

4. **Broken model.** Regardless of its power or resources, the effectiveness of risk management itself is often not critiqued or examined.

Complexity. Overlaps in risk management organizational structures increase confusion and exacerbate political turf battles.

10
FEAR INDICATOR 7 -
LEGAL DEPARTMENTS

"As I travel around the globe and meet with world leaders and other CEOs, the litigious culture of the US, the class-action culture — quite frankly, the ambulance chasing, the patent trolls — is what's being talked about."

— Bob Dudley, BP CEO

PAULA DEEN FOUND herself on a slippery slope — and not from butter. In 2013, reports of her racial slurs marked the culmination of a legal process that had started when an attorney for a previous employee had threatened not only legal action but to use that legal action to destroy her reputation. A Bloomberg Business article describes the situation:

Woolf offered Deen a choice. She could pay Jackson

$1.25 million or face a lawsuit. If Deen chose not
to settle, Woolf explained, he would seek maximum
news coverage. "Exposure of the racist and sexist
culture of her corporate and personal life is going to
permanently, and irreparably, damage the value of
her brand."

The incident was another powerful example of how the
US legal system has become a form of extortion. A form of
extortion that could never be attempted in any other context.
However, this practice is so commonplace that there is now a
new term for using the legal and political system to wage war
on an opponent: lawfare. By Wikipedia's definition:

A portmanteau of the words law and warfare, said
to describe a form of asymmetric warfare. Lawfare
is asserted by some to be the illegitimate use of
domestic or international law with the intention of
damaging an opponent, winning a public relations
victory, financially crippling an opponent, or tying up
the opponent's time so that they cannot pursue other
ventures. Other scholars see it more neutrally as a
reference to both positive and negative uses of law as
an instrument of warfare or even to the legal debates
surrounding national security and counterterrorism.

Yes, a system that was built to administer justice is now
increasingly used as a weapon of war to beat down an opponent regardless of what's right or just.

It's also being used to get rich. Attorneys looking for the
next payday, individuals avoiding labor in favor of a payout,
and businesses attacking each other using law firms instead of

product innovations. These are the natural byproducts of turning the law into a tool for one's own gain.

Over the past decade, there's been an explosion of firms specializing in outsourced legal marketing. These firms seek out individuals to add numbers and corresponding heft to class action lawsuits. They don't vet these "victims," nor do they have any altruistic goals of righting corporate wrongs. Rather, they want to prod businesses to settle for large sums — most of which gets funneled to partners in law firms.

It's a lucrative business in today's legal environment. As a *Bloomberg Business* article notes: [A law firm partner] calls lead generators "leeches on our industry" and says the prospective clients they identify often don't pan out. Still, he expects lead generators to proliferate, "because there's money to be made."

Or, depending on your perspective, money being wasted. In 2012 and 2013, Google's and Apple's combined spending on patent litigation exceeded $20 billion — far outstripping their investments in research and development. That big number alone illustrates how much our legal system contributes to fear-based business cultures.

It also illustrates that even market leaders can fall into fear of losing something they have. They're willing to engage in legal battles so as to squash any perceived threat to an existing cash cow. I am not saying that protecting key advances shouldn't be deployed — it only makes sense to expend some energy and resources on protecting what you have — but what return are Apple and Google getting on $20 billion? What advances could they have made with $20 billion? Return on investment is a concept that never appears to be present related to legal costs.

A significant portion of that $20 billion — along with many more billions expended by other tech companies — was likely related to "patent trolls" — businesses and individuals who buy older patents and sue very public companies who may have used a similar technology. Under the guise of patent infringement, it's a thinly veiled hope of getting a big and fast payday. For the cases that go to trial, over half end in a ruling in favor of the plaintiffs, making patent trolling a lucrative business even without considering settlements. A 2013 *Bloomberg Business* article notes the scope and scale of the practice:

> A White House report says more than 100,000 companies were threatened with infringement suits last year by businesses whose sole mission is to extract royalty revenue, and the Government Accountability Office says those outfits filed 19% of all patent lawsuits from 2007 to 2011. In cases that went to trial in 2012, licensors were awarded a median $11.2 million per case, according to a PricewaterhouseCoopers study.

To underscore the impact patent trolls have had on innovation, look at this 2014 chart from the *Harvard Business Review*.

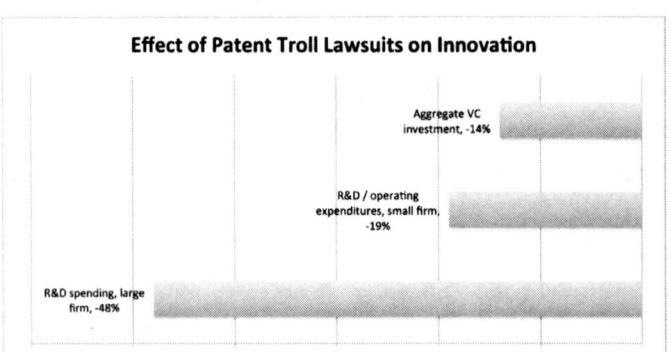

But maybe patents are the problem? Doubtful. The US Patent Office is largely considered to be the best in the world for protecting innovators. A *Time* magazine poll asked inventors, "Which countries do the best job of keeping your ideas yours?" 40% chose the US. The next closest country was Germany at 10%. The US patent system gives US inventors a huge advantage, yet the use of the legal system has managed to turn it into a weapon of fear.

That being said, many companies are beginning to fight back against patent trolls. The same 2013 *Bloomberg Business* article goes on to describe how:

> Google, Oracle, data-storage provider NetApp, and other tech companies have a new strategy for fighting back: petitioning the US Patent and Trademark Office to revoke the patents they're allegedly violating. These patent reviews, set up under the 2011 America Invents Act, can discourage frivolous patent claims by shifting the burden of proof to the plaintiff. The patent holder can't refuse a review, overseen by administrative patent judges, even if a court case is already in progress. The outcome of a proceeding, required within 12 months instead of years, is legally binding; and although the trial judge isn't required to put a case on hold while the Patent Office conducts a review, most do.

Ars Technica magazine notes a recent example. In 2013, a shell company called Lumen View Technology told Santa Barbara startup FindTheBest that it should pay $50,000 for infringing its patent on "multilateral decision-making." Instead of getting a quick payout, it ran into FindTheBest founder Kevin O'Connor and a Racketeer Influenced and Corrupt Organizations (RICO) lawsuit.

O'Connor said he'd re-focus on building his company, but will press forward with the RICO lawsuit. "If anything this is further proof," he's quoted as saying. "Their methods of extorting money from people are reprehensible and, we believe, criminal." It's a high bar, and previous attempts to pin down patent trolls with RICO have not succeeded, but the industry is clearly tiring of patent-based abuses of the legal system.

A New Legal Environment

Tech isn't the only industry affected — perhaps because there are more than enough lawyers go around, as a 2013 *Bloomberg Business* cover hammers home in its text: "What do you call 176,000 lawyers lying at the bottom of the ocean?" The cover article explains, "The Bureau of Labor Statistics estimates that during the decade ending in 2020, the US economy will create 73,600 lawyer positions. Law schools are pumping out 25,000 graduates a year, suggesting an excess of 176,400 J.D.s no one really needs." With this many lawyers, lawsuits are sure to follow.

Businesses have reacted in kind. For perspective on the expanding size and scope of legal departments and outside counsel within US corporations, consider the following:

- A 2013 survey found that a full 30% of larger US companies have at least 5 in-house counsel managing litigation — up from 21% two years prior. 18% have at least 20 lawyers performing this function.

- The percentage of large companies using outside counsel for help with governmental or regulatory investigations increased from 43% to 60% between 2010 and 2012.

- The top 200 corporate law departments in US companies employed 27,700 lawyers in 2006.

- The largest corporate law departments in US companies in 2006 were Citigroup (1,500 lawyers) and GE (1,200 lawyers).

As a result, litigation is ready for launch at a moment's notice. The medical field knows. The *Quarterly Journal of Economics* estimated recently that the practice of "defensive medicine" — doctors prescribing treatments, X-rays and life-support principally to pre-empt legal action — costs $50 billion per year. Put another way, fear is costing the medical profession $50 billion per year. That doesn't even count all the side effects of these unnecessary medicines and procedures, plus delayed treatments for those who really need them. Such waste seems preferable because the headaches of fighting malpractice are too painful.

A 2001 *Newsweek* article notes how the uniqueness of the US judicial system sows the seeds of fear:

> In some countries, people resort less readily to litigation because the courts could take decades to rule on a suit. In America, the profusion of lawyers (the country's most popular profession) and the existence of a well-honed judicial structure means no one has that disincentive. In fact, the

propensity of juries to award staggering damages encourages lawsuits.

The juries themselves add an interesting wrinkle to the legal landscape, as seen in a case involving the pharmaceutical company Merck. Merck was sued by thousands of consumers alleging that its painkiller Vioxx caused them to suffer heart attacks and strokes. The plaintiffs had evidence that Merck knew of the risk and downplayed it to regulators and the public. However, many plaintiffs also faced a serious hurdle in proving that it really was Vioxx — as opposed to factors like age, smoking, or obesity — that caused their injuries. In the US system, this question of individualized causation is a question for the jury.

The lawyers for the plaintiffs and Merck agreed to hold a series of "bellwether" jury trials to help figure out whether juries were likely to find that Vioxx caused particular plaintiffs to suffer heart attacks and strokes. And, although Merck won most of these sample trials outright, and although almost all of the jury verdicts won by plaintiffs were reversed on appeal, Merck nonetheless settled the case for nearly $5 billion. Fear of a larger jury decision steered their decision-making.

Sometimes even clear-cut evidence doesn't hold up. For years after the media storm around Toyota and a handful of cars that suddenly accelerated, hundreds of cases wound their way through the legal system — despite mounting information that Toyota was not at fault. "We enlisted the best and the brightest engineers to study Toyota's electronics systems, and the verdict is in," said Ray LaHood, then secretary of the US Department of Transportation. "There is no electronic-based cause for unintended high-speed acceleration in Toyotas."

The plaintiffs themselves seemed unable to produce evidence. Carly Schaffner, a Toyota spokeswoman, was quoted in the media as saying, "Despite nearly three years of litigating this case and unprecedented access to Toyota's source code, plaintiffs' counsels have never replicated unintended acceleration in a Toyota vehicle and have failed to demonstrate that any alleged defect actually caused the accident at issue in this case."

Yet a jury in Oklahoma determined that software in the electronic throttle system of a 2005 Camry was defectively designed, causing an accident in 2007 in which a 76-year-old driver was seriously injured and a passenger was killed. The jury awarded $3 million in compensatory damages and was considering punitive damages when Toyota agreed to a confidential settlement.

You could ask why a business has to defend itself against lawsuits even after NASA's rocket scientists give them the all clear, even when plaintiffs are unable to prove their case. In the face of the evidence, the damage was done — and not just by settlement payouts. Toyota's market share of the US auto market dropped from 18% to 13% after the complaints surfaced, rebounding only slightly to 14% or 15%.

The layers add up — the number of lawyers, the parties eager for reward, juries' propensity for large payouts, and investors' need for swift and full closure — and make it clear that a business has nearly no way to avoid a destructive situation. Is there any reason not to fear this legal environment?

But the intent of this chapter isn't to dwell on all that is wrong with the legal system. Rather, it's to understand how legal fear can influence decision-making. As is the case with all of the fear factors, their ability to create a culture of fear has less to do about the factors themselves and much more to do with how we as management respond with fear. Even legitimate business threats can be addressed in a manner that leads to sound business decisions and doesn't take your business outside its core values.

After all, the legal threat is real. Even with everything on their side, Toyota still suffered lost market share and costly settlements.

The net effect of our legal environment is that culturally we have swung the pendulum too far towards our legal advisors. The complexity leads us to become beholden to legal advice — which in many cases can be self-serving. Like that of risk management, compliance, and business strategy consultants discussed in previous chapters, legal advice can have the same intrinsic motivation to sell more of itself. And the threat of business failures is a very powerful sales tactic.

Michael Robinson, executive vice president at a crisis management firm, notes the fear-generating phenomenon of advice: "In 2013 big consumer-facing companies are risk-averse. There are so many voices now they have to pay attention to." Ultimately, these voices distract us from bravery.

Practically, the way we listen to these voices can be seen the common expectation of avoiding liability. Even around entertainment! Every year in men's college basketball, some home team David upsets a top-ranked Goliath. Inevitably, the students (and over-invested adults) come streaming onto the court. It's supposedly fun, but it's chaos. Players have physical run-ins with overzealous fans, and the masses invariably cause a handful of injuries among themselves.

Sports commentators show surprise that colleges and

universities haven't banned the practice for safety and liability reasons. As if they could snap their fingers and end it. Even if they add extra security personnel to the end of each aisle for late game situations or build barriers to prevent thousands of excited fans from storming the court, it just wouldn't work. And the costs would far exceed the outcome of any lawsuit.

Is it really negligent to not double or triple the police presence? No, but legal fear makes it almost assumed that organizations will invest resources to avoid any possible liability. And fearful organizations do. They consider it worth almost any extra cost to have the appearance of being proactive.

The National Football League (NFL) offers a current case of how litigation fear can affect a business. In the 2000s, reports began to surface about former players suffering dementia, depression, and other neurological diseases at alarming rates. The initial response by the NFL was to downplay the impact and to re-emphasize that these men knew the risks when they decided to play professional football.

However, as media attention grew stronger, more evidence emerged, possibly indicating that the NFL had actually hid the dangers. In response, the NFL began to overhaul its rules. Many of these changes were long overdue, like having any kind of concussion protocol. But most are clearly designed to give them some kind of legal standing. Fearing future lawsuits, they are focused on protecting themselves rather than on making good business decisions.

As it happens, many of the changes have altered the game. Penalties have gone up, players are expressing uncertainty about the rules, and even the public seems dissatisfied with the NFL's actions. As a result, the NFL has struggled with a public relations perception. Their handling of the issue has been seen as reactive at best and incompetent at worst. The popularity of the sport remains high, but the NFL's legal-minded behavior is starting to tarnish its appeal.

A New, Expanding Influence

For legal advice, most companies have a chief legal officer or general counsel. It is no coincidence that the term counsel is used, but, as the legal environment turns many businesses to be dependent on legal advice, the role often changes from counsel to leadership. As noted by the President and CEO of the American Corporate Council, Veta T. Richardson, "Fulfilling the dual role of business executive and legal advisor is the new normal for chief legal officers today."

A 2013 issue of *Today's Legal Council* characterizes the CLO's role evolution:

> The rise in salaries tracks the CLO's broader responsibilities, requiring business as well as legal acumen. The role of the CLO has evolved to include far more than the traditional duties of practicing law and setting legal policy for the organization. As members of the C-suite, CLOs are serving as strategic business partners and providing oversight in such areas as corporate governance and compliance and risk management, in an increasingly complex regulatory environment.

As the following chart shows, advising executives and corporate strategy is now a CLO's highest time allocation.

Chief Legal Officer –Time Allocation

**Please estimate how your time was allocated over the last 12 months.
(Responses must equal 100%.)**

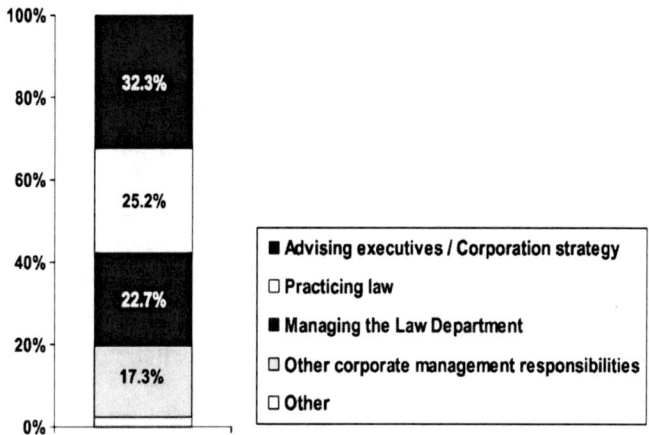

This expanding role has paid off for attorneys aspiring to be CEO. In 2010, 9 of the 50 Top S&P companies had a former general counsel as their CEO. Many attribute this to visibility. Boards tend to select only the people they know. Since the CEO, CFO, and GC are at every board meeting, they get the most exposure. But the complexity of regulation, risk/control, and globalization also give some edge to legal experts.

As CLOs and GCs rise toward the corner office, they may have an underlying handicap, as described in a *Bloomberg Business* article:

> Risk aversion can be another problem. People who go to law school rather than B-school tend to be more cautious. After all, they're choosing a career that holds out the prospect of a guaranteed good income

— rather than a small chance of a spectacular one. What's more, the main goal of business lawyers is not to maximize profits but to minimize danger. "Good CEOs have to be able to make tough, bold decisions in the face of uncertainty — and that's hard for lawyers," says James C. Gaither, a former corporate attorney who is a managing director at the Silicon Valley venture capital firm Sutter Hill Ventures. "Lawyers want to keep working until they find the perfect answer."

The *ABA Journal*, writing on this very phenomenon, talks about the rub of the GC's traditional role as defender compared to the CEO's perspective of making a balanced decision that is best for the business:

> But at the end of the day, the CEOs say there is only one thing that can place the general counsel in the line of succession: results. "The general counsel has to do more than just give a legal report. He or she needs to come up with business solutions to problems," Steiner says. "There are going to be plenty of times when we as lawyers are going to say no. But we need to be able to help the board find an answer."

This general trend of bringing the CLO, or comparable position, into the executive team has had unintended consequences. It provides a strictly legal viewpoint that can go unchecked by rational considerations, let alone brave decision-making. It can even inject fear directly into the heart of the organization.

Tim O'Reilly wrote about this recently, considering the

evolution of his employee handbook and the culture that it created:

> Eventually, I hired an employment lawyer to review my draft, and he said, "That's the most inspiring employee manual I've ever read, but I can't let you use it." I complained, but I eventually gave in. As we grew, it was harder and harder to maintain our informal processes. (I remember a real inflection point at about 50-60 employees, and another at about 100.) We gradually gave up our homegrown way of doing things, and accepted normal HR practices — vacation and sick days, regular reviews, annual salary adjustments — and bit by bit, I let the "HR professionals" take over the job of framing and managing the internal culture. That was a mistake.
>
> I've often regretted that I hadn't kept fighting with the lawyers, working harder to balance all the legal requirements (many of them well-intentioned but designed for a top-down command and control culture) with my vision of how a company really ought to work. I focused my energy on product, marketing, finance, and strategy, and didn't put enough time in to make sure I was building the organization I wanted.

These experiences occur in every organization and often lead managers to find ways to work around the legal teams. Legal teams are important and can be great resources as long as they serve their intended purposes rather than becoming the final say, a veritable dead end to any great business idea.

In 2013, *Fast Company* featured a great article on how Taco Bell partnered with Doritos to create the Doritos Locos Tacos. The article describes how they needed to avoid having the legal contract process get in the way of the development and rollout of the product. In the end, the leaders of the respective companies had to come together over a handshake agreement with a commitment to memorialize the agreement at some point in the future. The article quotes Greg Creed, then-CEO of Taco Bell, as saying, "Well, guess what, we sold 100 million tacos in the first 70 days. If we waited for those contracts to be finished, we would've sold 100 million less."

New Legal Advisors

The problem with business advisors in general — whether legal or accounting or risk management or business consultants — is that they are incentivized to keep themselves fully employed. Sometimes that means providing advice that is in their own best interests. Many times, that advice is not in the business's best interests.

A 2013 *Bloomberg Business* article examines the business consulting firm McKinsey. Many of its scathing critiques could apply to anyone in the business of peddling business advice, legal or otherwise:

> The McKinsey Man wasn't an expert in any one
> industry, but a generalist valuing rational thinking
> and blunt talk. McKinsey fostered a reputation
> for attracting fresh minds that weren't hampered
> by entrenched ways of thinking. Another way of

looking at this is that it hired inexperienced kids and forced them to learn on the job at the client's expense. This rarely became a problem, however, because the decision to hire McKinsey was typically made by a company's chief executive officer, the last person to admit that he'd made a rotten decision by hiring McKinsey.

As a former consultant at Arthur Andersen and a purchaser of consulting services in a large multinational insurance organization, I'm very familiar with the bravery it would take for a manager to call a consultant out and move on.

But it isn't enough that unchecked consulting firms have perpetuated fear in so many parts of our institutions. They continue to be pitched as our solution to a maddening new array of problems. A 2014 *The Economist* article discusses emerging solutions for disengaged and ineffective boards, pitching the idea of outsourcing the board to consulting firms:

> *Stanford Law Review* Stephen Bainbridge of the UCLA, and Todd Henderson of the University of Chicago offer a proposal for fixing boards that goes beyond tinkering: replace individual directors with professional-services firms. They argue for the creation of a new category of professional firms: BSPs or Board Service Providers. Companies would hire a company to provide it with "board services" in the same way that it hires law firms or management consultants. The BSP would not only supply the company with a full complement of board members. It would also furnish it with its collective expertise, from the ability to process huge quantities

of information to specialist advice on things such as mergers.

The professors offer no mention of the conflicts of interests this creates or how these conflicts of interest have led to many of the corporate scandals of recent decades — auditing firms selling consulting services that impair their independence, ratings agencies selling bond underwriting. With even greater influence on the board, these same firms would have little reason not to see their first priority as the best interests of the company but instead as selling additional services.

The underlying problem of these "solutions" is their uncritical esteem of experts. Noreena Hertz, a professor of economics at University College London, published an opinion piece in the *New York Times* about her life-threatening illness and the process of discovering the real cause and an appropriate treatment. Her essay doesn't reference business consultants, but her experience covers the concept of the need to evaluate outside advice:

> Physicians do get things wrong, remarkably often. Studies have shown that up to one in five patients are misdiagnosed. Yet people are loath to challenge experts. In a 2009 experiment carried out at Emory University, a group of adults was asked to make a decision while contemplating an expert's claims, in this case, a financial expert. A functional M.R.I. scanner gauged their brain activity as they did so. The results were extraordinary: when confronted with the expert, it was as if the independent decision-making parts of many subjects' brains pretty much switched

off. They simply ceded their power to decide to the expert.

Anxiety, stress and fear — emotions that are part and parcel of serious illness — can distort our choices. Stress makes us prone to tunnel vision, less likely to take in the information we need. Anxiety makes us more risk-averse than we would be regularly and more deferential.

We need to know how we are feeling. Mindfully acknowledging our feelings serves as an "emotional thermostat" that recalibrates our decision-making. It's not that we can't be anxious, it's that we need to acknowledge to ourselves that we are.

It is also crucial to ask probing questions not only of the experts but also of ourselves. This is because we bring into our decision-making process flaws and errors of our own. All of us show bias when it comes to what information we take in. We typically focus on anything that agrees with the outcome we want.

I chose a surgeon who wasn't overly confident. I'd learned in my research that the super-confident, doctor-as-god types did not always perform well. One study of radiologists, for example, reveals that those who perform poorly on diagnostic tests are also those most confident in their diagnostic prowess.

My surgery went well. The pain subsided, the pounds gradually came back on. I am now cured.

Note that she isn't saying to disregard advisors entirely.

She's simply saying to be reasonable and rational — exactly the approach that we need in the complex and sometimes irrational legal environment we have today.

Tort reform would be great. But let's be honest. Lawsuits aren't going away. They'll still be frequent, and their threat will be real and large for a long time.

What can change is our view of potential legal problems in relation to business decisions. We must develop a sense for real legal risk that isn't inflated by our perception biases or those of advisors, whether internal or external. Only then can we hope to work in a brave environment that frees our people to move forward with confidence rather than being fearful of the boogeyman of lawfare.

The Essex Revisited

Captain Pollard had advisors in the form of Joy and Chase. Despite having strong convictions regarding the best path forward, he deferred to the young guys because of fear. Consider this passage about avoiding the Marquesan islands:

Just as he had after the knockdown in the Gulf Stream, Pollard succumbed to them. "Not wishing to oppose where there was two against one," Nickerson remembered, "the captain reluctantly yielded to their arguments.". . . While rumors of cannibalism in the Marquesas were widespread, there was plenty of readily accessible information to the contrary.

Pollard let fear blind him to his own convictions, and he ceded authority to those to whom it did not rightfully belong. This theme plays out in organizations across America. Whether it is legal counsel, business consultants, risk managers, or just influential people, we don't always filter their advice and move bravely based on our convictions.

A quick recap of the fear factors around the legal system:

1. **Legal environment.** The environment dictates the size of the legal department, the amount of time and energy devoted to litigation, and ultimately the amount of influence the legal department has in day-to-day decision-making.

2. **Legal influence.** The amount of influence that high-ranking legal-focused individuals wield and their general attitudes in terms of taking on some legal risk for the sake of competitiveness.

Legal advisors. Not just the presence of outside advisors, but the level of specialization needed. Specialized firms have more incentive to use fear as a selling tactic to earn more work for themselves.

11
FEAR INDICATOR 8 - MEDIA & PUBLIC RELATIONS

"Fear's payday is frequently heightened panic, shaken confidence, and frantic decision-making."

— John Michael, Commanding General
NATO Air Command, Afghanistan

A 2013 TIME MAGAZINE article looks at the evolving thought process around menopause and the use of hormone treatments. The article — subtitled "The latest (but likely not the last) word on estrogen therapy" — examines study results over a 20-year period. In the 90s, doctors prescribed estrogen and progestin to treat menopausal symptoms and prevent heart disease. Then, a 2002 study revealed that long-term post-menopausal use of hormones increased risk of heart disease and breast cancer. Then, a 2004 study of women with hysterectomies showed taking estrogen alone did not lower their risk of heart disease but did have higher rates of stroke. Then, a 2013 study suggested that 50,000 women who avoided taking estrogen may have died prematurely.

And why did many of them avoid taking estrogen? Because of the media buzz around each new study.

Media: Sowing the Seeds of Fear

The media is the communications vehicle that gives a voice and credibility to many of the fear factors reviewed in the previous chapters. If I were to represent this interplay between the various factors, I would represent it as such:

(LRC)M = (Legal * Risk Mgmt * Compliance) ^ Media

With the diffusion of media outlets and influential blogs, social media accounts, and cable channels aimed at niche audiences, the equation carries an ever-larger influence — on both personal and organizational levels.

I have had a front-row seat to this explosion. In 2007, I started a local blog site called *Fort Thomas Matters*. Devoted to my community of Fort Thomas, Kentucky, it started as a response to a small businesses being forced to close. Larger media outlets seemed unaware of stories that smaller suburb communities really cared about. Over time, I added writers, and we posted multiple stories per day on events relevant to our community of 16,000 people. Within four years, we were averaging over 50,000 page views and had a Facebook page with thousands of active and engaged followers.

Amidst the success, I became exhausted by the pursuit of the next story. At times I even felt pressured to overplay or even invent new. That exact pressure has led to much of the current problem with our media environment today. My feelings of exhaustion with the media treadmill is summed up nicely by a post on the investment website The Motley Fool: "I've learned that journalists' need to write far exceeds the number of things that need to be written. No writer can say to their boss, 'There's nothing important to write about today,' although it is the truth most days."

Sure, too many experts with different agendas and different funding from sources are each advancing their own agendas. But it's the amplification of these conflicting studies in the 24-hour news cycle that truly sows the seeds of fear. Too much airtime and web content leads to republishing and sensationalizing the agendas and reports that hammer us with confusing and sometimes conflicting messages.

One personal "favorite" example was a story on a local Cincinnati news station. It ran for a week with promos warning of "deadly drop-offs" — read in a loud ominous voice with a near echo — and talked about slight differences in pavement height that had caused some recent accidents.

A more famous example was the Malaysian Airlines 370 flight. The strangeness of the situation was noteworthy and newsworthy, yes. But the coverage went well beyond the actual information:

> The executive acknowledged this was not really a
> story where reporters have been able to advance the
> known facts much. Instead, it has been fueled by
> a lot of expert analysis based on the little verifiable

information that has been available, speculation about what might have happened to the plane and where it might be now, accompanied by all the visual pizazz the network can bring to bear.

At one point the anchor Don Lemon used a toy model of the plane to illustrate a point being made by one of CNN's aviation experts. During another interview, Mr. Lemon raised the question of whether something otherworldly happened to the plane.

"Especially today, on a day when we deal with the supernatural, we go to church, the supernatural power of God," Mr. Lemon said. "People are saying to me, why aren't you talking about the possibility — and I'm just putting it out there — that something odd happened to this plane, something beyond our understanding?"

Commenters on social media over the last several days cited the toy plane as an especially egregious example of vamping instead of adding anything substantive to the coverage, along with a reliance on some commentators known more for chasing conspiracy theories than analyzing air disasters. Judy Muller, the former ABC correspondent who is now a professor of journalism at the University of Southern California, said: "I fear I am part of the problem. I keep tuning in to see if there are any new clues." She added, "Of course, endless speculation from talking heads soon defines the coverage and that can lead to the impression that these folks know something when what they really know is that they have a 20-minute segment to fill."

This hyperbolic tone of media coverage — especially when used to mask minimal amounts of information — can obviously skew any story.

Corporations recognize this. Media exposure, as a result, is often deeply feared. The bigger the company, the more they feel they have to lose from bad publicity — instead of seeing even crisis-type coverage as an opportunity to establish a different or stronger perception among their customers or potential customers

Tesla, a company I admittedly admire, knows and understands how to use this to its advantage. When they began to ramp up their production, the media took notice. They raised questions and doubts about how well the batteries would hold up in a serious high-speed impact crash. As a result, each crash that led to a fire was a headline-making news story. On October 1, 2013, when road debris punctured a battery on a car and led to a massive car fire, a passerby captured it and published it on YouTube. It was a lead on most major news outlets, and Tesla remained quiet on the incident for three days until the Founder and CEO, Elon Musk, published a blog post on the issue.

In the post, Musk highlights safety features — the on-board alert system directing the driver and occupants to exit the car, the firewalls between battery packs preventing the fire from reaching the cabin of the car. He discusses features — comparing the battery pack's quarter-inch armor plating to the thin metal sheet protecting a conventional car's gas tank. He examines safety statistics — showing the Model S to be roughly five times safer than a typical gasoline powered engine. He provides a copy of an email exchange with a more-than-satisfied customer.

Although there was pressure to rush out a response — even highlighted by a *Forbes* article that was posted along with video of the crash — Tesla was methodical in gathering all the facts. They created a clear, detailed description, added credibility to their message, and turned a potential negative into a massive selling opportunity by using the spotlight to showcase their product's superiority.

Going from Seeking Publicity to Protecting from Publicity

On February 12, 2014, Derek Jeter announced his retirement via a Facebook message encapsulating a love story between a great baseball player and the team, city, and sport that gave him so much. The well-written announcement received accolades across the media landscape for its expressive nature and authentic voice. It was a rare gem in a world that has carefully crafted messages written by PR firms and reviewed by 13 attorneys. There was no fear behind the message. No concerns about legacy and trying to shape, with one final statement, how history should view Derek Jeter. Just a heartfelt expression of a full career and a desire to grow in different ways as a person.

It reminded me of another conversation about public relations and the media today. This conversation also happened in the world of sports, and more specifically also baseball. Mike

& Mike's morning show on ESPN Radio was honoring the Hall of Fame baseball player Tony Gwynn after his passing. One story was how he treated a young boy in his teens who had created a small magazine and was growing it out of his basement. Gwynn embraced this young man and even introduced him to a writer from the *New York Times*, leading to his eventual hiring.

The hosts of the show, Mike Greenberg and Mike Golic, used this example to talk about how differently today's athletes approach the media. Golic made the point that the shift appeared to occur when PR departments went from seeking publicity for their clients to protecting them from publicity.

The same psychology exists in many business organizations. Senior managers and executives, when scarred by past experiences where negative publicity has hurt sales, often avoid publicity entirely. It is the equivalent of throwing the baby out with the bath water. Even though a clear public relations strategy can create an immense amount of goodwill for a brand, some companies refuse to engage the media for fear of negative publicity.

This fearful way of thinking can be exacerbated when reputational risk has a high degree of importance to the company — especially in industries like financial services, healthcare, or pharmaceuticals. When you buy insurance, you buy a promise. When you deposit funds at a bank, you trust them with your money. These industries are especially susceptible to extra doses of fear when it comes to engaging the media or seeking publicity for your company.

But when companies in these industries don't engage the media, develop relationships with members of the media, and shape the message they want the public to hear and understand, they risk reacting to messages that others put out. This reactivity puts any organization at two inherent disadvantages. First, the other competing message is already out in the wild, often leaving the most lasting impression. The second is that, without having built good will, the organization can't depend on others coming to their defense or looking at the other message more critically.

So if taking a laissez faire approach could leave you in a defensive position, what is the right approach?

Taking Back the Conversation

We all know Apple. Considering that their success has been driven heavily by public perception, it's worth examining their methods. I wouldn't endorse all their tactics — I would even say some of their tactics could have even been birthed out of fear — but they're clearly doing many things right.

Most of the information in this section comes from the website 9to5Mac.com, a website devoted to breaking technology news from all the big players in Silicon Valley. The site's growing influence in terms of shaping the public knowledge of Apple as a company is seen in its massive audience that generates in excess of 500,000 page views per day.

The team at 9to5Mac.com did an in-depth look at the Apple public relations approach. It can provide a template for any business looking to take back their messaging. For context, at the time of writing, there were around 30 PR employees in Apple's Cupertino offices, plus another few dozen individuals scattered around the world to organize events, translate press releases, and either answer or dodge questions from journalists in every time zone. Apple handles its PR and Communications strategies wholly in-house — which, as discussed in other chapters, can help keep advisor-based fear from encroaching on corporate strategy.

Some highlights from the 9to5Mac.com analysis:

1. One of the primary things that Apple is known for is its keynote address. It is one of the primary ways that Apple communicates to the world and has been revered in its efficiency and delivery. The process starts weeks before keynote addresses. Apple's Public Relations, Communications, and Marketing teams keep an eye on media reports to determine expectations, leaking information to temper expectations that won't be matched by the announcements. Executives typically practice for two weeks, and senior PR members prepare special white booklets with the desired communication to be handed out to the rest of the Communications Group prior to the main event.

2. Around the same time as this meeting, Apple sends out invitations to special guests, that include a small group of Apple employees, reporters from major news outlets including *Bloomberg News*, *The New York Times*, *Reuters*, and *The Wall Street Journal*, and a small group of reliably positive bloggers. Apple's biggest boosters get early tips to expect and publicize the invitations.

3. Apple also has a little-known Momentum and Buzz Marketing team that is made up of a handful of people responsible for integrating Apple's products into popular culture. For instance, the team works with major sports leagues to integrate the iPad into coaching toolkits, helps music events integrate iPads into festivities, and gets organizations to deploy iBeacon-integrated apps for attendees. When a brand new device shows up on a TV show before it's in stores, Momentum was involved in making that happen.

4. Apple PR views themselves as being an "overall watchdog," monitoring what the media is saying about the company every day. This oversight is so important to Apple that a few times a week, top executives are sent a document detailing the company's latest press coverage. When Apple is not pleased with coverage, it sometimes works to shift the narrative, even attempting to undermine giant news organizations.

5. Apple's PR department presents a cool, measured public-facing image: it only responds to press inquiries when it wants to, doesn't offer quotes unless they'll be reprinted without criticism, and responds directly only when it determines that something needs to be said by "Apple" rather than "sources familiar with the matter."

6. Other writers say that Apple will indirectly confirm or deny claims by sharing an analysis of the past track record of the particular author who originally wrote a

story in question. These discussions can be helpful or stifling for the writer, but they're generally all positive for Apple, which has the opportunity to shape what's said.

7. In past years, Steve Jobs and Katie Cotton would meet with magazine publishers and big-name newspaper journalists to talk about Apple's plans. Since the discussions were completely off-the-record, the "information would be useless," according to a person with knowledge of the meetings. Yet these editors still were being given "insight into the company," which led to glowing profiles of Apple.

8. One reporter who covers a number of technology companies opined that "the huge difference is that people love Apple, and Apple PR knows it." With that in mind, Apple "understands that they're giving [journalists] a favor," says Lam. "Apple knows it has something other journalists want," another reporter says, "the plays are the same [as other companies'] but the motivations are different."

9. Also likely contributing to which publications get early access to products is the nature of pre-coverage — angles taken by writers during the product rumors cycle. As Brian Lam put it, "Apple can already tell what a review is going to say from [a publication's] pre-coverage, and they're not going to give you a review unit if you're not going to play ball." In other

words, Apple feeds the writers who will do its bidding, and starves the ones who won't follow its messaging.

The big upshot: Apple does any and everything to control the conversation.

The totality of our communications is the external manifestation of who we are — and it's bigger than just what we say. Throughout *Corporate Bravery*, we have talked often about core values and about how hiring and management practices should reinforce those core values. Any misalignment between these elements lets fear creep into your organizational culture.

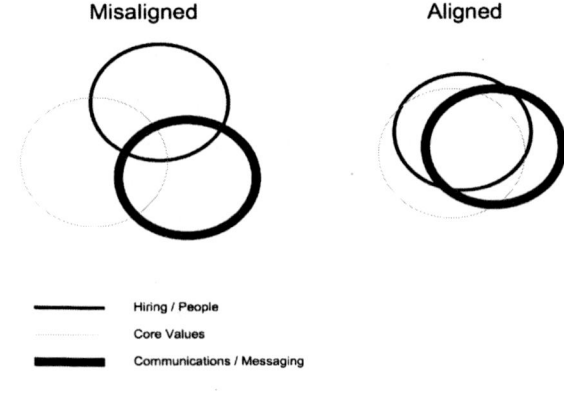

Misaligned   Aligned

——— Hiring / People
······· Core Values
▬▬▬ Communications / Messaging

You can never have 100% alignment between these three important organizational elements, but brave organizations have a level of consistency between them that communicates trust and authenticity. More often than not customers walk away with positive experiences and emotions with a brave and aligned company. Conversely, fearful organizations can occasionally get lucky and in some location or operating division there will be alignment and excellent performance.

To see how this manifests, let's contrast the former sister companies McDonald's and Chipotle.

	McDonalds	Chipotle
Mission	Be our customers' favorite place and way to eat and drink.	Change the way people think about and eat fast food
Tagline	I'm Lovin' It	Food with Integrity
Advertising	Saturated television advertising, billboards for travelers.	Little to no traditional advertising, use of web video to appeal to sensibilities around natural foods and sustainability.
Operations	Built for efficiency, utilizing technology to speed food delivery and drive through times.	Open kitchen, cooked to order, prepared in front of the customer.
Hiring / People	According to Glass Door average wages are $7.81/hr	According to Glass Door average wages are $8.57/hr

McDonald's claims to care most about an enjoyable place for people to eat, but their stores are built for efficiency. The emphasis is on serving the next customer as fast as possible. The dining rooms are not exactly warm and inviting. With high turnover rates, the employees are not typically welcoming either. As for the food, a recent *Consumer Reports* study notes, "At chains with the highest scores for food, 42% to 54% of patrons called the fare excellent, but at Burger King, KFC, McDonald's, and Taco Bell, no more than 11% of patrons did."

In 2014, *The Wall Street Journal* published experts' thoughts on McDonald's strategy. Comments include:

Larry Light, CEO of management consulting company Arcature: "In the short term, the first priority is to love the customers you have. I am concerned that the McDonald's strategy seems to be more focused on customers they would love to have. Attracting new customers is an imperative, but keeping current customers is the base upon which customer attraction yields incremental growth. Protecting the base is about never sacrificing the core principles that made the brand successful, and one of those in fast food is speed. McDonald's core customer wants fast service."

Carl Chang, founder and CEO of fast casual pizza chain Pieology Pizzeria: "I would embrace what McDonald's is and try to reinvent the brand. I have to give Mr. Thompson credit for trying to evolve the brand, but to re-identify McDonald's as a fast casual concept rather than what we've grown to appreciate McDonald's for — consistent, fast food — seems like a really bold move."

These inconsistencies were evident to the board and investors as well. Then-CEO Donald Thompson was fired in early 2015, just a couple months after his turnaround plan was announced.

On the other hand, Chipotle's consistency has raised the food quality expectations of fast food customers — and raised the loyalty of their customers. A 2014 *Fast Company* article shows one way their mission informs their decisions:

> In what it calls "blackout" situations, Chipotle puts up signs in affected stores announcing that the normal meat supply is unavailable and that traditionally-sourced meat is being substituted in its place. Does this decision make Ells a hypocrite, a leader who sacrifices his mission to maximize financial rewards? The way Ells sees it, his mission actually dictates this course of action. The more successful Chipotle is, Ells argues, the more resources they have over time to encourage farmers to adhere to their standards and increase the integrity of the food supply. Turning away customers could impede that larger goal. Customers appreciate that we're letting them know it's conventionally raised meats and the vast majority still order it anyway. Does this mean they don't care about our mission? No. I think they are happy that we're committed to serving better food. To not serve chicken means that there's not an economic engine that's making it possible to build up a supply of antibiotic-free meat.

While that is the CEO's perspective, what do customers actually think? From the same *Consumer Reports* study: "Chipotle Mexican Grill ranked at the top of their category, and offered speedy and solicitous service that the industry giants couldn't match."

Given this contrast in execution on mission and messaging, it's clear which business has alignment on the three factors of value, personnel, and messaging. It is this last one where misalignment becomes most apparent — people see through advertising that's inconsistent with their actual experiences and perceptions of what a company's actual core beliefs are.

Unlike advertising, nothing offers direct communication from your company's own voice like social media. All other forms of communication — outside of actual purchase and service interactions with an employee — are one-way. Not social media. With social media and two-way communication, anyone can have a dialogue with brand. That can be scary for companies without a solid core of people who represent their stated values — their social media messaging may confuse or offend customers or potential customers. It's tricky to control those conversations.

Fear of two-way communication is only amplified by the countless examples of a lower-level staffer — manning social media channel despite little understanding of or regard for the company's voice — putting the company's foot in its mouth:

- KitchenAid community manager. During a presidential debate, this confused employee thought that their personal offensive tweet about President Obama's deceased grandmother just went out to their small following. Instead, it was blasted out to over 24,000 of KitchenAid's followers.

- Kenneth Cole's insensitive tweet about their product in relation to the Arab spring protests in Egypt — which eventually resulted in deaths.

- K-Mart including promotion hashtags in their tweet

about the tragic events in the Newtown, Conn., school shooting.

- DiGiorno trying to use the conversation of the #WhyIStayed hashtag about domestic violence as an opportunity to sell pizza.

Each high-profile example leads to headlines like "DiGiorno's Unfortunate Hashtag Is Why Brands Shouldn't Be Allowed To Tweet" — a sentiment based in fear. The message is avoid doing something that could cause harm rather than understanding what led to the issue.

But for all the mishaps, there are also social media success stories — sometimes born from a seeming disaster. Take this sports drink example.

During the first game of the 2014 NBA Finals, the air conditioning in the arena failed. Temperatures in the arena rose above 100 degrees, but they played anyway. In the second half, league MVP Lebron James cramped up and had to sit out during crucial plays. With the best player in the league on the bench, his team lost.

What fans noticed, however, was the logo behind the cramping player: Gatorade. Almost immediately, they took to social media to rip Gatorade as a rehydration drink. What they weren't noticing was that James was a sponsor for Gatorade's competitor Powerade. This could have been a reputation-destroying situation for Gatorade, but what happened next was an excellent example of how to take back control. Gatorade responded to each tweet with a funny, snarky, or just matter-of fact-comment about how, had he been drinking Gatorade, James may have avoided the whole situation.

Gatorade @Gatorade 9h
@jkahn24 Thanks for being on our team.

36   57

Gatorade @Gatorade 9h
@dufresne33 Hydration definitely would've helped.

166   87

Gatorade @Gatorade 9h
@CarmichaelDave This is awkward....We don't sponsor him. #fail

1,032   763

Gatorade @Gatorade 9h
@LazyBumDrew we were waiting on the sidelines, but he prefers to drink something else.

1,462   758

Screen shot example of some of the tweets sent by Gatorade on June 5, 2014

Gatorade sent about a dozen tweets during an hour. Instead of getting beat by other people's narrative, they became the story. They later apologized to Lebron, but they had already accomplished what they set out to do — to take back control of the conversation.

Interestingly, small companies are 40% more likely than large enterprises to have someone in charge of their content marketing. They understand this power of social media to connect with customers and control the conversation. While not engaging in social media is often attributed to a lack of understanding, is that really any different from simply operating under fear?

Promoting Positive Emotional Connections

One school of thought around branding says that a lack of confidence in a brand is driven by insecurity. Confidence, on the other hand, is driven by feelings of safety and acceptance. As a result, organizations that want to create confidence optimize relationships with consumers by presenting a positive image. In turn, they promote safety and acceptance while downplaying feelings of insecurity.

But if that's true, why do so many brands play to fear? It seems there should be ways to create confidence without presenting a product or service as the way to avoid a terrible calamity.

Creating opportunities for consumers to believe is a powerful way of connecting. Since over 50% of a customer's experience is how they feel, you must be sure that your experience has a positive emotional component. When your customers feel a positive emotion connected to your business, you will create an emotional signature, which is part of your emotional brand image.

According to customer experience author Colin Shaw of Beyond Philosophy, it is important that you make sure that your organization is clear on your emotional brand image:

Usually we try to have our clients narrow this down into one word and then focus on how to make the word translate into the customer experience. For example, if your organization's word is trustworthy, make sure that your customer experience instills a lot of confidence in your ability to meet customers' expectations (i.e. if you say you'll do something by a date, it is done by that date, and so on). By engaging your customers' emotions, you can create a belief that it is time to spend again.

Interestingly, this is exactly the opposite of the way the media often propagates its stories. Which might be why distrust of the media is at an all-time high.

So what's our net situation? We seem to be letting courtroom-worthy theatrics sway our emotions. True facts don't win the day. It's whoever sways the public's mind the best.

Remember the Toyota acceleration issue in the previous chapter? That same story has played out in the media many times over in the automotive world alone. The Suzuki Samurai rollover threat in the early 90s (sales fell from 83,314 units to just 5,031 after the Consumer Reports story ran), exploding Crown Victorias in Dallas, the Firestone and Ford Explorer rollover controversy, and the Audi 5000 acceleration issue — all these disastrous consequences came after runaway media stories.

As a result, companies that are successful handling the media are the ones committed to leading the conversation. They create an emotional connection with their customers and society at-large by having a clear idea of who they are, hiring people who reinforce and behave consistently with those values, and communicating those values through words, actions, and experiences. By bravely leading the conversation, these companies aren't buffeted by competition — or by the latest media hype.

The Essex Revisited

Obviously, the Nantucket whaling industry didn't have media like we do today, but it did have a form of media that was just as powerful — the tales, fables, and rumors that masqueraded as truth:

Nantucket was, like any seafaring town of the period, a community obsessed with omens and signs, such a reputation counted for much. As a result, children's bedtime stories at night centered on tales of killing sea creatures and eluding cannibals.

> Still, there was talk among the men on the wharves when earlier that July, as the *Essex* was being repaired and outfitted, a comet appeared in the night sky. At the wharves and shipping offices there was much speculation, and not just about the comet. All spring and summer there had been sightings up and down the New England coast of what the Mercury described as "an extraordinary sea animal" — a serpent with black, horse like eyes and a fifty-foot body resembling a string of barrels.

As if comets and sea monsters weren't enough, other signs fed this general frenzy of fear:

That night he was probably unaware of the latest

bit of gossip circulating through town — of the strange goings-on out on the Commons. Swarms of grasshoppers had begun to appear in the turnip fields. "[T]he whole face of the earth has been spotted with them...," Obed Macy would write. "[N]o person living ever knew them so numerous." A comet in July and now a plague of locusts?"

This infatuation with the supernatural no doubt implanted itself in the back of the minds of Joy and Chase, making them want to avoid the island cannibals at all costs. The media of the day fueled the perception biases that led to fateful, fear-based decisions.

A quick recap of the fear factors around media and public relations:

1. **Media**. Businesses operate in a massive profusion of media outlets — many of them new media companies — seeking to break a big story, often through sensationalism.

2. **Going from Seeking Publicity to Protecting from Publicity**. Businesses have gone from an offensive position to a defensive posture, often thanks to encounters with the media that have ended negatively or fears about coverage eroding trust in a highly trust-based industry. This defensive posture causes businesses to miss out on opportunities for good press.

3. **Taking Back the Conversation**. Social media can be very scary for those that haven't aligned core, people,

and message in a way that is consistent. Any confusion between the three elements of clear communication can lead to confusing messages and give rise to fear.

12
CONDUCTING
BUSINESS BOLDLY

"Courage is knowing what not to fear."

— Plato

T O GET A high-level view on fear, let's return to astronaut Chris Hadfield and his TED Talk. As someone who's been literally out of this world, he has a unique perspective on real versus imagined fears, considering the probability of catastrophic failures are one in nine in his work. About overcoming fears, he says:

> What are you afraid of? Spiders? A brown recluse?"
> That is one of the most venomous spiders in the
> world, which can kill horribly. But it turns out
> there's only one venomous spider in Vancouver, the
> black widow. And it isn't fatal, and it mostly hides,

uninterested in humans. So what do you do if you're afraid of a spider? Walk into the next spiderweb you see. Take a good look and make sure it's not a black widow, and walk into it. Then do it again. I guarantee if you walk into 100 spiderwebs, you will have changed your fundamental human behavior.... And you can apply this to anything.

The idea of facing your fears by hitting them head-on in a controlled way works great for fear of spiders, heights, and darkness, but how does it play out in a business context?

One way is to embrace failure, an approach that is starting to gain traction among business authors. As quoted in *Fast Company*, Michael A. Roberto, trustee professor of management at Bryant University, sees the trend as a rebuttal to today's work environment: "A backlash has emerged because so many corporate cultures have become so intolerant of experimentation, and people have become so afraid to fail that they have become reluctant to try new things."

While the movement is seen as a backlash, it can have powerful implications on changing fear cultures within our organizations.

People are slowly realizing that the world is complex and that social, economic, and environmental factors make it impossible to predict and understand the future. Trying to control all those factors and expecting that failure of some kind shouldn't happen is an unrealistic goal. Which means fear of failure is needless.

In the same article, Mel Fugate, associate professor of management and organizations in the Cox School of Business at Southern Methodist University, suggests:

"Mistakes will be made — in research labs, management consulting teams, C-suites, factory floors, farms, hospitals, school systems, government offices, supermarkets, and elsewhere," she says. "So figuring out how to learn from failure is more important than ever before."… "Continual experimentation is the new normal," she says. "With risk comes failure. You cannot elevate the level of risk-taking without helping people make sense of failure, and to some extent, feel safe with failure."

You've heard executives say it's okay to fail in their organization. But when pushed to provide examples, they usually fall silent. Actions and words are often incongruent in the area of failure, and very few organizations know how to do it in a productive way that leads their employees to success at an individual performance level or their organizations to success through improved long-term performance.

The challenge managers face is how to encourage risk-taking and innovation without actually incentivizing bad outcomes. Fugate says the successful embrace of failure in the workplace not only requires a change in how performance is defined and rewarded, but also a radical mindset shift.

This is why a cultural revolution must occur within our organizations to alleviate the role that fear plays in decision-making.

Beginning the Transformation

To this point, we have largely focused on the ways corporate culture can be distorted and negatively influenced by fear. Chances are, you've formed thoughts about where your company, non-profit, department, or division sits on the spectrum of fear. You may have even declared your organization fearful or brave. Your assessment is likely right, but I want to give you a tool to quantify it.

Here's a short survey to determine not only where your organization stands but also where fear has been able to set up some strongholds.

http://www.corporatebravery.com/bravery-survey.html'

Use the results from this survey to begin the cultural transformation processes in the last three chapters.

No, really! Go take the survey now so we can use the same language!

Now that you have taken the survey, you have results for all three areas. The graphic below links the eight fear factors from Chapters 4 through 11 with a process for restoring bravery in each area.

This process begins by reprogramming the core — the fear factors around Management, Individuality, and Corporate Politics. You likely have a low bravery score in this category if there is mistrust among management and employees, if your mission and values aren't clearly defined, or if those values are not aligned with personal interests and desires.

In Chapter 13, we'll discuss ways that you can reprogram the core of your business to transform your organizational culture into a brave organization where managers understand how to take risks in a way that adds value without demoralizing your workforce.

The second component of transformation involves refocusing how we view external factors — the fear factors of Competition, Regulation, and Media. You likely have a low bravery score in this category if management in your organization takes a reactionary response to every possible perceived threat. This is acutely visible as it relates to news stories, competitive threats, or hints of new regulations.

In Chapter 14, we'll discuss ways to refocus how you view external factors that you have no control over. The main thrust of this conversation involves staking out a position for how you engage these external entities, establishing a leadership position for how your story is being told, being a market leader, and participating in the legislative process to position your company as an influencer.

The third and final transformation is improving decision-making — the fear factors of Risk Management and Legal Practices. Organizations that have a strong core and are directing external factors find it easier to make brave decisions than those that are fear-based. You likely have a low score in this area if consultants, risk managers, and attorneys have an out-size influence on day-to-day decision-making.

In Chapter 15, we'll discuss how to improve decision-making in a way that empowers front-line employees and managers to make decisions with confidence rather than being distracted by fears that distort outcomes.

13
REPROGRAMMING THE CORE

"I remember we were in New Zealand and I must have been 10, but I was nervous to go down this slide. That's when I started to realize that fear holds you back. So I went to the school diving board every lunchtime and jumped off the 1-m, 3-m, and 5-m board to get over it. Now I have no fear, which is probably a bad thing."

— Hugh Jackman

WHEN WE TALK reprogramming the core, there is no better analogy than the human body, where there are many great examples of amazing transformations. Some transformations happen out of necessity. A body ravaged by heart disease or cancer needs drastic changes — improved diet, more regular exercise, and possible medications and/or supplements.

Other transformations happen somewhat unnaturally — surgeries, enhancements, or chemical substances like steroids. The problem with those is that they often don't stand the test of time. Only through working with your body as it is — through discipline and hard work — can train and develop muscles and organs to perform at a higher level.

The body, in fact, is built for reprogramming, even down to the cellular level. Physically, reprogramming can come through workouts. Mentally, it can happen through education. Emotionally, it can come through relationships or therapy.

We're also susceptible to environmental factors. Being infected by viruses and bacteria or suffering an injury can — and usually does — happen to everyone. But our bodies frequently withstand these external factors. That is why diet and exercise are so important. Daily disciplines that strengthen the core improve our survival, not to mention attitudes and sheer enjoyment of life.

An organization is like a body. Many factors can make us more susceptible to being unsuccessful. As humans, we may not be able to improve upon or positively impact our genetic situation, we can be aware of it and ensure our behaviors help. In an organization, we have the power to change both structural issues and behaviors. We can't just write a check and solve them, but they can be fixed.

To outline some of the disciplines that strengthen our core and make us better able to respond to fearful situations, let's revisit the three related fear factors.

The Three Factors Revisited

Chapters 4, 5, and 6 talk about components of fear — individuality, management, and politics — that represent the core of a corporate culture. To rebuild the core, we have to start with addressing the ways that the toxic culture was created in these areas. In much the same way that we have to go beyond treating the symptoms to ensuring that the body is able to ward off viruses, bacteria, and disease, we have to make sure our organizations are healthy and able to withstand things that can prevent us from achieving our goals.

Individuality

Much of our focus in the chapter on individuality is on how a lack of respect for individuals within an organization can breed fear. Here, we focus on how a clear organizational identity contributes to a sense of belonging for the individuals within it, keeping fear at bay.

Workers everywhere are longing for a sense of identity. A 2013 survey by The Energy Project, a workplace consulting company, shows that three of the most important factors that employees feel are missing from their workplace are level of meaning/significance, connection to their company's mission, and a sense of community. The full results are shown in this chart from the *New York Times*.

White-Collar Salt Mine

A 2013 survey of 12,115 workers worldwide found that many lacked a fulfilling workplace.

DO NOT HAVE THIS AT WORK			DO HAVE THIS
70%	Regular time for creative or strategic thinking	18%	
66	Ability to focus on one thing at a time	21	
60	Opportunities to do what is most enjoyed	33	
50	Level of meaning and significance	36	
50	Connection to your company's mission	25	
49	A sense of community	35	
48	Opportunities for learning and growth	38	
47	Opportunities to do what you do best	36	
46	Ability to prioritize your tasks	36	
45	Overall positive energy	36	
43	Understanding of how to be successful	40	
40	Ability to balance work and home life	37	
40	Ability to disengage from work	42	
40	Comfort in truly being yourself	45	

94 percent of those surveyed were in white-collar jobs; 6 percent were in blue-collar jobs.
Source: The Energy Project

The results show that a full 50% of participants lack a connection to their company's mission. Coincidentally, only 25% felt they did have a connection, which means another 25% who don't even understand the concept. This is a big problem, since that's one major thing that employees want.

According to Ellevate, a global professional women's network of thousands of women, employees will push companies toward greater "meaning and purpose." When Ellevate asked their members about their priorities for accepting a job, the number one answer was "meaning and purpose."

Some workplace studies have found that employees who derive meaning and significance from their work are more than three times as likely to stay with their organizations — the highest single impact of any variable in the survey. These employees also reported 1.7 times higher job satisfaction and they were 1.4 times more engaged at work. As the Indian philosopher Patanjali said, "When you are inspired by some great purpose, all your thoughts break their bonds." Given that a significant portion of time is spent working at an organization, why would people not expect to have purpose in their work?

A clear purpose also contributes to trust. A *Harvard Business Review* article entitled "Why a Quarter of Americans Don't Trust Their Employers" discusses keys that predict more than half the variance in trust between employees and their organizations. At the top of the list is the employees' perception of the level of involvement they have in their organization. Second is how the organization communicates.

While it may seem like the level of involvement and communication are somewhat unrelated to purpose, there is a close correlation. Organizations that have a clear purpose usually communicate well and therefore communicate their purpose well. Chances are, there are leaders who are constantly communicating where the company is headed and why, increasing the level of involvement that employees feel they have towards that purpose or mission.

Every organization must find an identity. Whether you are a unit, department, or division leader you have the power to impact this. Each team has an identity, a unique culture that is all their own. Communicating that identity is crucial.

At Epipheo, our organizational success is built off the ideas generated by our creative staff, about two-thirds of our employees, while I oversee all the administrative functions. When I started at Epipheo, the focus was on leading the finance and accounting teams, but I began to piece together a department of people who, though doing great work, were isolated. They didn't feel they were part of a team and didn't have a group of people that could encourage and support them.

After a year, we brought IT, HR, Finance & Accounting, and Administration into one group, all with the goal of supporting our customers — all the other employees. Suddenly, we had an identity that allowed us to feel we were each a more integral part of the bigger picture and driving results.

Doug Connant, the former CEO of Campbell's Soup and now a leadership consultant, stressed the importance of having a clear organizational identity: "When you are in the stormy seas of decision-making, having a deep and abiding sense of what matters most to you is mission critical."

That certainty helps get through potentially fearful moments. A new product release from a competitor. Changing regulatory landscape. Difficult relationships. A deep and abiding sense or purpose — clearly communicated and aligned with your personal mission and beliefs — can make decision-making easy even in hard situations.

No matter what culture exists, a strong sense of purpose allows individuals to feel respected and have a sense of belonging. When this happens, management can stop focusing on superficial things in the organizational context and instead focus on how each person adds value to the whole organization.

As important as organizational identity is, however, it's not enough in itself. If you have hired the wrong people for your culture, it can be easy to drift away from that central core or have it muddied.

The critical link to avoiding this situation is through strong and thorough hiring practices. At Zappos, after a new employee goes through training, they are presented with "the offer" — $4,000, on the spot, right then, if they quit. This ensures that whoever stays isn't staying for the paycheck. They're staying because they love the company, and really want to work there.

It is up to the organization to force the prospective employee to confront their individual fit. Too many organizations expect that the recruit will ask the right questions or, from limited interactions with one or two employees, make that determination themselves. The most important thing you can do in hiring and recruiting is be clear about who the organization is, prodding recruits to ask themselves how it aligns with their own values.

Hiring processes must emphasize desired behaviors to give candidates opportunity to self-select into (or out of) an organization's culture. Disney does this in a variety of ways, specifically by casting a story of how each individual's role fits in the context of the company and how that role is expected to be performed. Disney uses pre-hire media to set up both the candidate and organization for success. These materials define standards and expectations via demonstrated behavior. Here are some examples of the ads they use to appeal to bus driver candidates.

It is clear to prospective bus drivers that they have an important role to play at the parks. What is a seemingly low-level job has been elevated, and the message is clear — you won't fit in this role if you are just looking to punch the clock and collect a paycheck.

At Epipheo, we do a 90-day trial period. Employees are hired with the expectation that nothing is guaranteed, so it's opportunity both for the employee to check out if it's a place they want to work and for the company to make sure the fit is right in both culture and competence. At our regular all-company meetings, we celebrate whenever someone completes their first 90 days and becomes "one of us."

Chris Zook, in his book *Repeatability*, writes about embedding clear non-negotiables into a company's cultural fabric:

> In the typical company, only about 40% of employees say that they know the strategy and its priorities. Imagine if this were true of a football team or marching band. We found that successful companies like IKEA or Nike capture the key ideas of their strategy in few key principles and beliefs that we call non-negotiables, and embed them in critical routines on the front line. This ensures that the company's strategy is translated into front line action — the very place where most strategies fail.
>
> Take Vanguard, the largest mutual fund company in the world. Vanguard's non-negotiable principles include not being able to beat the market in the long run and the primacy of investor loyalty. These non-negotiables shape Vanguard's differentiation and

translate to front line behaviors. Everyone from the CEO to a customer rep in the call center can describe them using similar pride and similar words. Vanguard has clarity of message that any political candidate would envy. When customers voted, in effect, with their cash during the financial crisis, Vanguard received more than 40% of all investment funds in the US.

In short, individuality has to be ensured and guarded bravely by both the leadership and the individual.

Management

In Tony Wagner's bestselling book, *Creating Innovators: The Making of Young People Who will Change the World*, he notes that "the average child asks 100 questions a day, but by the time a child is 10 or 12, he or she has figured out that it's much more important to get right answers than to keep asking thoughtful questions."

While we aren't administering standardized testing in our corporations, we do often reinforce that there are right and wrong approaches, behaviors, and attitudes for success — and that failure isn't one of them. This is one of the deepest fears in our organizations.

Much of Chapter 4 focuses on the relationship individuals have with their boss — and, more importantly, how that relationship can create an environment where failure isn't an option. But to be a successful organization, you must create a culture that not only allows failure but possibly even embraces and celebrates it. When that happens, people feel comfortable to take risks, to step out, and to embrace challenges. They are freed up for personal growth — and, therefore, excellence — in the role they were hired for.

That starts by establishing trust through good communication. As there are many ways to erode trust, there are many ways to build it, primarily through being authentic and honest. There are also many ways to communicate well within an organization. We won't enumerate all of these approaches but rather focus on the end-game — building a brave culture that allows or even encourages people to take risks.

Most organizations focus on resolving defects and failures. Think about all the people and resources devoted to quality, process improvement, or Six Sigma. These are all well-meaning activities and are necessary to maintain value for the end consumer. But think about the language of these organizations — "zero defects," "preventable occurrences," and, above all, "fail-safe." All phrases that indicate the organization doesn't tolerate failure.

Management scholar Jennifer Mueller has studied creative assessment and found hidden cognitive factors at its core, as quoted by *Co.Design*:

> There are situational variables that are very subtle
> and transitory that can shift your ability to determine
> what's creative. These seemingly random factors —
> such as a manager's mindset during an idea pitch
> — can bias people against creativity without them
> knowing it.

In one study, published in *Psychological Science* last year, Mueller and collaborators asked test participants to rate a creative product: a running shoe equipped with nanotechnology that improved its fit and reduced blistering. Some of the participants were put in the mindset of someone open to uncertainty — by being told there were many potential answers to a problem. Others were put in frame of mind that favored certainty — told that a problem needed a single, certain resolution.

These slight mental nudges had an outsize effect on assessments. Participants who'd been predisposed toward certainty rated the shoe as significantly *less* creative than those predisposed to tolerate uncertainty. They also responded more favorably to concepts of practicality on an implicit word association test. The researchers concluded that idea evaluators can harbor a "negative bias against creativity" they don't even realize exists.

Just the very nature of corporate environments — the structural compositions of hierarchy, functional roles, policies and attitudes towards various business practices — can create an environment that kills creativity.

So how do these negative biases come into being? It comes back to the personal relationships we focused on in Chapter 4. The erosion of trust between employees and management keeps employees from being free to contribute their best thoughts and their best work.

In order to rebuild the core of your organization, you must assess the team of managers that has been assembled to carry out the mission of your business. In keeping with our biological analogy, if your employees are the muscular system, then your management team is the nervous system.

When that nervous system isn't working in concert with the muscles, your organization suffers. It is a form of organizational Parkinson's disease. It develops gradually, sometimes starting with barely noticeable tremors. Then, beyond the growing tremors, the disorder causes stiffness and slowing of movement. You are left with an organization that is not only inefficient but is literally fighting itself.

To keep the core strong, you need to perform a top-to-bottom assessment of your managers. It is common for the CEO or leadership team to assess the management team from time to time, but these assessments are often flawed performance review templates based on technical proficiency, annual performance goals, tenure, or how likeable they are.

Instead, the assessment should focus on how well the manager represents the company's values, how well they are doing at establishing trust with their employees, and how well they are creating an environment where employees feel empowered to take risks and operate fully in the strengths that they bring to the organization.

What do you do after the assessment? The hard work: determining who can be developed and who needs to be re-assigned or, perhaps, fired. Yes, I used the "f-word" — fired. This may seem harsh, but some managers are a real disease to an organization's nervous system and need to be removed. This, of course, won't apply to most managers. The more likely scenario is that managers — who often still have technical or institutional knowledge that is highly valued — get re-assigned to non-managerial roles.

Focused attention and development should be given only to the managers who show signs of brave, skillful leadership and embody the values of the organization.

Corporate Politics

In a culture that allows failure and has a healthy political environment, managers and high performers do not have to worry about having failure used against them.

One way to create a healthy political culture is to promote understanding across divisions, departments, and groups. This can be difficult when also trying to promote group identity, as noted above, but it's essential.

According to Dr. John Sullivan, a management professor at San Francisco State University, people don't naturally move throughout an organization because of several reasons: lack of information about possible opportunities, managers hoarding talent, appearance of disloyalty, fear of rejection, insufficient time to prepare for opportunities, no career focus, and corporate restrictions.

Regardless of the reasons why this movement doesn't happen naturally, a culture must value it and actively work to make it happen. That also means that it can't just be an HR initiative, but something that managers in all parts of the business embrace.

An aggressive rotation program of high performers can help create cross-division understanding. Moving people through the organization builds a base of high-performing employees in all departments, divisions, and business units. These high performers not only understand what other divisions are trying to accomplish but can even champion opportunities in other areas — even opportunities that require sacrifices in their own divisions. The rotation program helps them see what the organization truly needs.

When it comes to turning politics into a force for good instead of fear, it is also a good time to come back to Chapter 3's thoughts on how ownership amplifies fear.

THE FEAR CYCLE

I recommend we move from ownership to stewardship. We need people who can buy into the greater purpose, not own a piece of it. Motivated for that purpose, they'll be willing to view their role as a steward of the entire organization, not an owner of a particular part.

An ownership mentality leads managers to create fiefdoms and battle to protect them, creating a negative political environment. Stewards, however, see all parts of the organization as an important part of the whole, each needing support so the entire organization can excel.

The stewardship approach improves attitudes toward team members as well. Owner mentalities view employees as opportunities to leverage for bigger and better titles and pay. Stewards, however, view their people not as headcount but as people who have aspirations. Stewards work with them to develop them and improve their performance.

While it is important to hire employees and managers who think like stewards rather than owners naturally, it is just as important to set the tone for stewardship at the highest levels of the organization. Often, this begins with having a purpose beyond profit. Is the mission and vision compelling enough for employees to want to be stewards? Is it compelling enough to invest in emotionally? Or will the absence of a compelling mission and vision allow employees to revert back to a sense of ownership?

What is certain is that a steward-led organization will not get caught in political battles. Rather, its people will work bravely towards compromise because what is best for the organization is what they believe in and want to support.

Building Capacity for Grittiness

During recessions, people ask whether healthy organizations have suffered any damage. The answer: yes. Even powerful organizations are at the whim of larger things. Even companies that did all the right things had to make tough decisions. What sets them apart, however, is not what they did. It's how they did it. The best organizations found ways to do tough things in ways that were healthy, fair, and as transparent as possible. It's not that the bad stuff didn't happen. It just happened better for the company and better for people involved.

In Andrew Zolli's book *Resilience: Why Things Bounce Back*, he defines resilience as "the ability of people, communities, and systems to maintain their core purpose and integrity among unforeseen shocks and surprises."

For Zolli, resilience is a dynamic combination of optimism, creativity, and confidence. Together, they empower one to re-appraise situations and regulate emotion — a behavior many social scientists refer to as "hardiness" or "grit."

Margaret Perlis, a former executive and a writer for *Forbes*, has praised grit, too:

> While courage is hard to measure, it is directly proportional to your level of grit. More specifically, your ability to manage fear of failure is imperative and a predictor of success. The supremely gritty are not afraid to tank, but rather embrace it as part of a process. They understand that there are valuable lessons in defeat and that the vulnerability of perseverance is requisite for high achievement.
>
> As I noted in a recent post, courage is like a muscle; it has to be exercised daily. If you do, it will grow; ignored, it will atrophy. Courage helps fuel grit; the two are symbiotic, feeding into and off of each other... and you need to manage each and how they are functioning together.
>
> The courageous aren't seeking to fail, but they know

failure is part of a natural, healthy process. Their grit kicks in after they have acted on a decision. There are only two possible outcomes, so they fight like hell to make sure their outcome is success. In that moment, the ability to think clearly, to calmly make the right calls, and to rally their people to victory — those abilities define their grittiness.

Paul G. Stoltz, Ph.D., author of the book *GRIT: The New Science of What it Takes to Persevere, Flourish, Succeed*, defines four components of grit as:

- Growth — your propensity to seek and consider new ideas, additional alternatives, different approaches, and fresh perspectives.

- Instinct — your propensity to pursue the right goals in the best-possible ways.

- Tenacity — The degree and duration of relentless effort and energy you put into whatever you do is tenacity.

- Resilience — How well you respond to adversity and your capacity to be strengthened and improved by the tough stuff.

It is the resilience portion of grit that can be shaped by how you respond to fear. Acting fearlessly means you have to be resilient. If you are, you'll develop a mental capacity that lets you adapt with ease when things don't go your way. Like bamboo, resilient types bend but rarely break. You also have to let go. That ability to let go drives a constant process of change. It's what makes people flexible and adaptable.

The problem is that America has lost some resilience. That cultural context has affected our organizations' ability to be courageous. What it requires is that we rebuild our core — not just to recapture that grittiness but to strengthen our ability to make good business decisions that propel us to sustained growth.

To bring it back to physiology, think of a patient-doctor relationship. There is a general recognition that medicine has placed too heavy an emphasis on immunization or medication to solve health problems. An over-reliance on antibiotics can be long-term harmful on our body's ability to fight off illness effectively because it isn't paying attention to overall health. It's too focused on individual dangers.

This same mindset is pervasive in our business organizations. We build business plans that count on a moderate amount of growth, and we work like hell to accomplish individual goals linked to this plan. As long as we hit those goals, the problems with our core go un-noticed. Our cultures are rotting away. Only when we have problems delivering on a plan do we recognize the cultural problems that have been simmering just below the surface.

Management has likely been relying on the easy medicine of organizational changes, budget reallocations, or incentive modifications. In reality, they should be pumping the daily cultural iron of trust, communication, and creativity. As these will bring health to individuality, management, and politics, they will also build up an entire grittiness of culture that can withstand the shocks rather than falling into fear-based decision-making.

14
REFOCUSING HOW
YOU VIEW EXTERNAL
FACTORS

"If there is fear, there is a reason — our job is to find the reason and to remedy it. Management's job is not to prevent risk but to build the ability to recover."

— Ed Catmull, President, Pixar

FEAR MANIPULATES OUR perspective. It can make us think that any situation is the result of external factors we fear. It is easier to blame external factors — a certain co-worker, the competition's latest product enhancement, or the economy — than to look at our own inability to process a situation correctly. This clouded judgment is a direct result of our fears.

The Berkshire Hathaway annual report, historically written

by Warren Buffett and his partner Charlie Munger, is widely regarded as a must-read. The 2012 annual report discusses the Berkshire Hathaway approach to external factors as opposed to the typical business executive:

> There was a lot of hand-wringing last year among CEOs who cried "uncertainty" when faced with capital-allocation decisions (despite many of their businesses having enjoyed record levels of both earnings and cash). At Berkshire, we didn't share their fears, instead spending a record $9.8 billion on plant and equipment in 2012, about 88% of it in the United States. That's 19% more than we spent in 2011, our previous high. Charlie and I love investing large sums in worthwhile projects, whatever the pundits are saying.

Blaming external factors often leads us to deny reality rather than face it head on. This denial causes us to believe a series of self-imposed lies about our ability to positively influence outcomes:

- Following the crowd is the logical choice out of the situation we are in.

- The future is the most important thing, preventing us from dealing with the present realities.

- The future will play out as it has in the past, preventing us from considering all options by forcing us to try something new.

While blaming the competition, the media, or regulators may galvanize your workforce toward a common enemy, it isn't productive and doesn't provide a solution. Eventually, your staff get disillusioned with this lack of plan and grow concerned about the future.

Safety is Important, Just Not How We Typically Think of Safety

In a 2014 TED Talk, author Simon Sinek discusses safety by providing examples of courage and bravery within the military.

He tells the story of a commander in the Army fighting in Afghanistan. Under enemy fire, he's loading wounded soldiers onto a medevac helicopter. The scene is captured on a GoPro camera being worn by a medic. In the footage, the commander is kissing the men as he loads them into the helicopter. Sinek asks, "What is it about leaders like this? Leaders who have teammates who say they would do something because they would do it for their leader?"

According to Sinek, it's the environment. Specifically, if the organizational environment is right, then we all have the capacity to sacrifice for others the way they do for us, creating a deep sense of trust and cooperation. It is a culture that relies on feelings, not instructions. When we felt safe among our own, we develop trust.

The word safety does not mean a sense of certainty. Rather, it means believing that leaders and peers have our best interests at heart and are in the battle with us against any external threat.

We shouldn't desire a safety that prevents pain. We are not meant to not feel pain. Pain spurs us on to make changes and do better. Not feeling pain, in fact, is unhealthy.

I grew up in church, often hearing Bible stories about the dreaded disease of leprosy. Only recently, however, did I learn how those afflicted with the disease lost extremities. It was not because of the disease itself. It was because of an inability to feel pain. From repeated, unnoticed injuries, lepers would lose parts of their bodies. Pain isn't the problem.

Yet, in many organizations, managers have a mindset regarding safety that makes them try to insulate their people from making mistakes, either to avoid pain for themselves or for their people. In reality, safety isn't about not feeling pain. It's about knowing that, when those situations arise, those around us and above us will be there to help us learn what caused the pain, then to put the appropriate protections in place to be successful the next time.

A *Wall Street Journal* article entitled "You're Awesome! Firms Scrap Negative Feedback" describes how e-commerce company Wayfair teaches its managers how to make feedback "palatable" so that the company's hundreds of young workers not only understand they are doing a great job but exactly what it is they're doing great. The problem in this approach isn't giving positive feedback. It's in shielding people from the truth of hard realities. Over time, this "safety" only serves to weaken performance and cause harm — not only to immediate performance, but also to the employee's long-term career prospects. And, of course, to the corporate culture.

The key, then, is to build and ultimately stand confidently when confronted with various external factors. Fear is given permission to cause great harm when we don't have the confidence to know to not grow anxious or move from our position of strength. But when we think of pain as a tool to help us grow, we don't have to falter in the face of fear.

Of course, we can't just conjure up confidence. It only comes from knowledge and real world experiences we can draw upon. The problem is that our universities and corporate learning groups do little to teach managers how to react emotionally to difficult business situations. Our managers rarely put their people in positions where they are able to grow through real world experiences that can teach this important skill.

The Center for Creative Leadership (CCL), a global provider of leadership development that has ranked among the world's Top 10 providers of executive education, has coined a rule for leadership development — the 70-20-10 rule. It indicates that successful leaders learn within three clusters of experience. 70% comes from challenging assignments, followed by 20% through developmental relationships (e.g. mentoring), and the remaining 10% coming through classroom style training.

CCL's work underscores the importance of being willing and even creating opportunities for managers to stretch themselves — possibly at the risk of failure — in order to build successful leaders.

In the web series *Capture Your Flag*, Global Campus founder Maurizio de Franciscis was asked, "How did participating in the GE Management program shape your leadership style?" His response:

I realized that being able to accomplish things is not

necessarily correlated with being the smartest person in the room but it is almost more about being resolute and being resilient. It was interesting because I had to jump from one business to another at GE, every six months I would be sent to another country working in another business and taking on one or two or more of the problems on the table of the CEO. I would land and they would say here are my problems, which one do you want to take and then I would normally take one or two and in one business I took six or seven and you run with that. It's very interesting because it's high exposure and high scope situation in a sense the ability to make mistakes without being burnt because even if you do something totally stupid you will move away from their business anyway — they won't hate you forever and that it is still somebody else's decision to implement or not. So it's almost like trial and error being a CEO and in that, the leadership course is great.

GE understands the effectiveness of the 70-20-10 rule and went all in on it decades ago. Today, they are known as one of, if not the best, management training organizations in the world.

Mentoring As Therapy

The other important component of the 70-20-10 rule is an area that often goes overlooked: mentoring. While 70% of S&P 500 companies have a mentoring program, these programs often are ineffective.

Mentoring acts as a form of corporate therapy, relying on a trusted third party who's free from political considerations and truly has everyone's best interests at heart. Much like how only a trained professional can help someone work through anxiety and depression, a mentor can do the same for employees affected by fear in decision-making.

Progressive companies that have been doing mentoring well are even embedding the process further with peer mentoring and reverse-generational mentoring. These organizations understand that having an independent third party to work through issues compliments the "challenging assignments" that are so critical for growth.

Fortune magazine chronicled the growth in peer mentoring. A 2012 article attributes this growth to a 50% increase in reports that managers handle. Companies like Microsoft and KPMG have developed programs in which peers from different divisions or locations mentor each other to provide fresh ideas about career paths, help employees develop new skills, and keep them engaged with their colleagues and the company in general.

Much like therapy, the article notes that "the mentor-mentee relationship should evolve into a form of sponsorship. As bonds form, the connection should evolve from that of a coach, who tells you what to do, to that of a mentor, who offers advice, to that of a sponsor, who advocates for you."

This is consistent with the stewardship mentality I advocated for in the previous chapter. Hiring stewards instead of managers will raise the effectiveness of even informal mentorship inside your organization. So much so that it will likely be more effective than many of the best-run formal mentoring programs. Stewards understand that they have contributions to make even outside their direct responsibilities. But, to a steward, such additional investment is natural.

Internal Behaviors to Combat External Threats

You may be wondering why I'm focusing so much on internal processes when this chapter is about external threats. Well, fears are internal experiences. The idea that there are things "out there" that create universal fear experiences is false. Many people, myself included, are scared to death of snakes. Others have them as pets and let them roam freely around their home. Fear doesn't come out of the snake. Rather, fear comes from what we believe about the snake.

Armed with this knowledge, whenever we notice an internal fear response, we can process each step leading to the fear, then disassociate the pain from the thing or event. Once we understand that pain is something we create, we can take responsibility for our thoughts and feelings and choose to feel differently about it. Having separated our feelings from the actual external activity, we are now in a position to make a rational decision instead of one based out of fear.

There is a concept in education called the zone of proximal development, depicted in the figure below. At the core of this concept is the idea that we all start in a comfort zone. This is where an individual can learn independently and develop skills and capabilities without assistance. Just outside of that comfort zone is a region where development can be accelerated by the right coaching, development, and training — and, crucially, being in situations where you may even learn from failing. Outside of that is a zone that is simply beyond us. Its challenges are too advanced.

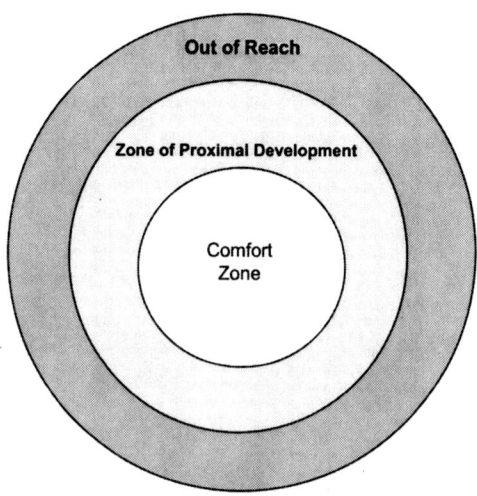

The problem is that our corporations are not pushing us sufficiently away from our comfort zones. They often view zones of proximal development as Out of Reach zones rather than appreciating how productive they can be. As a result, we find ourselves stuck in the comfort zone, building up barriers of fear to avoid moving out of it, and failing to grow or learn.

Brave companies, on the other hand, create systematic ways to move employees into the zone of development. This isn't simply to counteract fear, but to encourage growth. The satisfaction that comes from this development process will foster bravery as a general disposition, leading to employees who are not afraid to take calculated risks or look for opportunities to lead a rather than following the crowd.

Use External Factors to Your Advantage

Armed with a deep and abiding sense of who you are through maintaining a strong core, and with the support of a community inside your organization — formal mentoring relationships and/or supportive management giving you stretch assignments — you are now poised not only to not fear external threats, but in fact to take advantage of them as opportunities to build a leadership position for your organization.

Let's take a look at the three external fear factors again in the context of keeping your mind in check from irrational fears.

Media

It always amazes me when I hear corporate executives using phrases like "keep our heads down" or "lay low" (which is grammatically wrong anyway). I understand that working with the media can feel like warfare, but making statements like these should be a gut check about the ethics with which you conduct your business. If there is truly something to fear from media coverage, then you're likely operating at the edge of what the community finds acceptable. That concern should be a wake-up call to rethink how your business works.

All media coverage is good media coverage. I'm not suggesting you should be the Kardashians of your industry, nor that you should relish negative headlines. But you should view the media as an opportunity to shape the story. Although it might take some work.

Elizabeth Macbride, writing in *Forbes* magazine, shares a writer's point of view:

> When I was working for *Crain's New York* as the managing editor, I worked on a story with the great reporter, Louise Kramer, about one of Leona Helmsley's hotels. It was a rough story: The hotel hadn't upgraded in a while, and there were customer complaints. When [the story] was over, Louise got a package in the mail: a giant stuffed version of Trouble, the lap dog to whom Helmsley later left her fortune. The note read something like this, "All media is good media. Thank you."
>
> …
>
> Sometimes, even when the story isn't perfect, you have to engage. If you're in the middle of a bad story that the media has uncovered, you have very little choice *but* to engage, in a limited fashion. And it will help the future. A better approach than trying to hide something unsavory is to frame a short, truthful story that puts the episode in the context of your company's entire stream of accomplishments.

The key, clearly, is not "keeping your head down." It's not acting out of fear. It's having the bravery to engage with the media and take control of the story.

Competition

Similarly, when you are being ruled by fear of the competition, the tendency is to put your head in the sand and stay chained to your desk. But the brave action is to stay close to the customer, out from the protection of the office. Not only to hear their needs but to adapt your products and services to meet their needs by understanding them better — better than before and better than the competition.

That process won't be painless. You'll hear some difficult things. But being close to your market's needs is the best way to stay on offense and avoid chasing the competition. A scared posture only leads to a losing strategy, taking you off the cultural center of why you became important to your customers to begin with.

But it isn't enough to just hear your customers' concerns. You also have to translate them into action. The best way to do that is by making room for product innovation. A process to collect this feedback, prioritize opportunities, determine which most play to your strengths, and then assign resources to make it happen. These are offense-minded approaches to meeting those customer needs, letting you lead the market rather than follow the competition.

A fearful manager says, "Look at what they're doing, then go copy it." A brave manager says, "Look at ourselves, then do what we do better." Don't be tempted by the easy play. It will often take you off mission and lead you to poor results.

Regulation

As with the media and competition, the key attitude about regulation is to be proactive, not reactive. Get out in front of legislation by understanding where regulatory momentum is headed. Stake out a position that is not only in alignment with that new landscape but is leading and providing the example for your market.

For example, consider the minimum wage. Every five to ten years, we have a national discussion about it. There's always an economic reason behind the discussion, and it's just a matter of time before a higher minimum wage becomes a national law. And yet, many companies always fight it.

On the other hand, a few brave companies come to grips with this eventuality and use it as an opportunity to score some media and public relations wins. A recent example is the health insurer Aetna. While the national minimum wage was $7.25 per hour, they increased their company's minimum wage to $16 per hour. The move prompted big headlines such as "Aetna Lifts the National Standard for Competitive Pay." In that *Wall Street Journal* article, the move is praised:

> Amid signs of a tightening labor market, Aetna Inc. plans to boost the incomes of its lowest-paid workers by as much as a third in a bid to draw top prospects and reduce turnover. Around 12% of Aetna's domestic work force will see a raise to a floor of $16 an hour, primarily employees in customer service and billing-related jobs.
>
> Aetna Chief Executive Mark T. Bertolini said the company's shift reflects changes in the insurance

industry, which is increasingly selling coverage to individuals. "We're preparing our company for a future where we're going to have a much more consumer-oriented business," he said, and Aetna wants "a better and more informed work force."

Aetna, in this example, is actually managing all three external factors that we've discussed. They show leadership with regard to regulation. They use the media to control the conversation. They let their core values steer them as a leader against their competitors, not a follower. By not allowing internal fear to control their decisions, they're able to demonstrate bravery in the face of multiple external factors.

15
IMPROVING
DECISION-MAKING

"I learned that courage was not the absence of fear, but the triumph over it. The brave man is not he who does not feel afraid, but he who conquers fear."

— Nelson Mandela

WHILE LEGAL AND risk management were the two main fear factors discussed, there are literally hundreds, if not thousands, of factors that have the ability to impact decision-making.

In fact, we just spent eight chapters talking about a multitude of ways that fear can be spread in your organization. The reality is that, above all, competing interests among hundreds or thousands of influences, strategies, and pressures ultimately affect decision-making. All of these competing interests can create an environment of analysis paralysis. So this chapter won't break down the two particular factors like the previous two did for their respective factors.

Thousands of books have been written on the decision-making process. Personally, I've heard dozens of corporate training programs on decision-making, and I don't intend to try and recreate that here. There are more than enough concepts or resources to help you screen competing priorities.

Unfortunately, these books on decision-making rarely talk about the one thing that prevents us from actually pulling the trigger on that great decision: fear. It is hard enough to balance competing priorities without the influence of fear, so fear's presence only increases the complexity of the decision-making process exponentially.

What I intend to do here is to help you eliminate fear from your decision-making process so you can step into the decision in a bold way, ready to take responsibility for its outcome — whether positive or negative.

In her TED Talk on hard choices, professor Ruth Chang describes our decision-making processes:

> We should focus on where we want to go and who we want to be and view hard choices as an opportunity to reinforce that rather than let the world dictate who we are. If we see the choices as equally good or a little better/worse, then we let things like fear or complacency write our story for us.

There is a reason that we started the fear eradication process with rebuilding our core rather than talking about decision-making. Once we are certain what our organization is, what we stand for, what values are most important — and have hired people that not only are those things but reinforce them with their daily actions — only then we can be certain that we're making decisions that move us toward our ultimate goal or vision. Otherwise, without that foundation, there's always the chance that our decisions are pulling us away from what we should be and where we should be going.

But, even though you're aware of the factors that sow the seeds of fear within the business context — and even if you've already worked on rebuilding a strong sense of who you are as an organization and put external influences into their proper place — you still have to make the decisions.

We can talk endlessly about theories behind our fears and how to avoid falling victim to them. Ultimately, to make that theory pay off, you have to put yourself in a situation where fear can't unduly influence your decisions. That is what this chapter is about.

Clear Up Confused Authority

Our organizational structures depend on authority. Some organizations, like the military, understand this and have very clear lines of authority. These lines are reinforced through customs like salutes, uniforms, and rank. It is critical for the military to have clear lines of authority. When things get chaotic, and life or death decisions need to made quickly, everyone needs to know who's giving the order so everyone can then act swiftly to carry it out.

Our business organizations have lost this sense of

authority. Either because managers or executives have confused it or because they have chosen not to live into that authority in a full and meaningful way.

During my last year at the insurance company, we dealt with an incredibly difficult and somewhat ambiguous compliance issue. There was a lot of focus on it, not only within our company but also from the parent company as well. As a result, a lot of people were involved in the process. My boss and the chief underwriter were both executive sponsors, creating a confusing shared authority. My boss would talk as though he was advocating on behalf of our team, but he would always acquiesce to the chief underwriter, implying that the real authority was with the chief underwriter.

Beyond that particularly confusing authority, many other voices spoke out during meetings. One such voice was a corporate attorney. Hierarchically, he was a peer. But he was given implied authority equal to or even exceeding that of the executive sponsors. This implied authority gave the attorney the confidence to behave unprofessionally on many occasions, even making personal attacks. The project manager and I went to the executive sponsors to talk about his behavior. We asked them to rein him in, and they assured us that they would do so.

During a meeting two weeks later, I disagreed with the attorney. He immediately went on a tirade, including a string of profanities directed at me. As he become more and more red-faced with anger, the executive sponsors sat silently. As it was clear that the reins were entirely off, I gathered my things and walked out of the meeting.

The executive sponsors had not lived up fully to their

authority and had even acceded an implied authority to the attorney, confusing the decision-making process and leaving the team an ineffective and dysfunctional mess. A short time later, the project manager and I both left the organization.

Managers and executives should have power to make decisions and to be leaders of people. However, most organizations have confused this authority so badly that fear seeps in. As a result, many people who shouldn't have authority can act with great amounts of implied authority.

To be a brave organization, take back the authority. Look around your organization. Take stock of those who are living fully into their authority — not in an abusive way, but those who have garnered the respect of their people. They're able to mobilize their people to great performance. It's a fine line between authority that is lorded over subordinates and authority that is earned out of respect for sound decision-making, vision, and leadership. And it is usually easy to spot the difference between the two.

Recently, my hometown witnessed an example of this need for clarity in authority. The *Cincinnati Enquirer* ran an article about a memo the chief had sent to the entire Cincinnati Police Department regarding the casualness of the department. The memo says, "Regardless of rank, all personnel should begin their correspondence to the chief with 'Sir' or 'Chief.' All correspondences should end with 'Respectfully' or 'Respectfully Submitted.'"

On the surface, attention to detail is something that should be commended and pursued in high performing organizations. But a "chief" who has to command people to use official titles — to say nothing of the fact that the memo was leaked to the press — clearly holds a lack of respect and inability to live up to his full authority.

Authority has negative connotations in our culture, but it is absolutely necessary. I am not advocating for a militaristic command and control culture that doesn't fit with the work environment most American workers are pursuing. Rather, I suggest it's crucial for managers to know the authority they have — and must use — to lead, coach, and make decisions for the best interests of both their people and their organization.

More importantly, that authority must not be confused. Clear lines of authority might seem harsh, but, when they're lacking, it only gives others implied power, creating a sense of fear among those they're supposed to be leading.

Learn How to Have Constructive Debate

Ron Ashkenas, a managing partner of Schaffer Consulting and co-author of *The GE Work-Out* and *The Boundaryless Organization*, explains (in a *Harvard Business Review* article) one frequent hindrance to decision-making:

> When a company's planning and decision-making
> process involves a lot of meetings, discussions,
> committees, PowerPoint decks, emails, and
> announcements, but very few hard-and-fast
> agreements, I call that "decision spin". Decisions
> bounce around the company, from group to group,
> up and down the hierarchy and across the matrix,
> their details and consequences changing as different
> stakeholders weigh in. Often, the underlying problem

isn't an inability to make decisions — it's a tendency to avoid conflict.

While much of this decision spin is a symptom of the authority issue just discussed, decision spin doesn't prevent decisions from being made altogether. But it does prevent decisions from sticking, because people hesitate to express their disagreements during the discussion. All the head nodding, smiling, and camaraderie is undermined later when participants don't follow through on decisions they didn't really buy into.

The first reason for avoiding conflict is that managers are people and have a very human desire to be liked. They want others to think well of them, and they want to get along and seem like team players. Even when they disagree with something, they often hold back on expressing it too strongly so as not to get into a fight. In fact, many managers are afraid that disagreements might turn into uncomfortable battles that will damage or destabilize relationships. They unconsciously pull their punches to keep things calm.

However, healthy debate can be constructive as long as everyone knows that it is supported as a means for achieving the best possible outcome. For that understanding to exist, everyone must believe that the collective wisdom of the group is better than any one individual and have a shared respect for the strengths that each other brings to the table.

The second reason for avoiding conflict is that many managers lack the skills to engage in it constructively. They must be humble enough to talk to each other after heated exchanges and reinforce that they still respect each other, emphasizing that, while they may have disagreed on this one point, nothing is changed on a personal level. Speaking of which, they must also stay above personal attacks.

I've spent entire tenures at companies without ever having someone, after a disagreement, come to me and say they respected my perspective. That isn't even necessarily humbling themselves. It is simply a recognition that we aren't enemies and that we can still find common ground and be advocates for each other. But when that recognition doesn't happen, I might think we are enemies, bringing fear into my own decision-making.

Managers must also be skilled at managing the debate and know when to cut the discussion off. Perhaps it becomes too heated, perhaps it starts to get personal. Managers must know exactly when to step in and protect constructive working relationships.

Ask New Questions

For leaders in an organization, one of the most important skills to develop is deciphering the motivation behind resistance to a new idea or concept. Often, this resistance comes from either a desire to avoid disrupting routines or fear of losing control. Good leaders work to overcome those resistances.

One way they do so is by asking broader questions prior to big meetings. Instead of jumping right into analysis of a new product or initiative, they dispel fears. Much decision-making focuses on the details — the size of the market, what the marketing plan could look like, potential partners, or the financial commitment — but these details can create uncertainty and fear. To set the tone and put people in a more visionary mind-set, ask a set of questions intended to open everyone's mind or frame the discussion.

In his book *A More Beautiful Question*, Warren Berger has this to say about helpful questions that can generate the decision-making outcomes that everyone will buy into:

Fields told me he doesn't particularly like the *What if you could not fail* question because "it proposes a fantasy scenario. I'm more interested in taking people through a series of questions that will actually empower you to take action in the face of the reality that you might fail." Fields suggests that we use questioning to confront failure head-on by asking:

What if I fail — how will I recover? The psychiatrist and author Judith Beck told me that she uses a similar question with patients — *If the worst happens, how could I cope?* — because, as she explained, "People's anxiety goes down once they realize they will live through their worst fear, and that they have internal and external resources that will help them get through it."

What if I do nothing? The point being, when we take on a major challenge it's often because we really need to change — and if we don't go ahead with it, we're likely to be unhappy staying put.

What if I succeed? "That's important because the way our brains are wired, we tend to automatically go toward the negative scenario. So in order to give your mind a chance to latch on to something positive, something that will actually fuel action rather than paralysis, it's helpful to create some level of clarity around what success in this endeavor would look like."

What's truly worth doing, whether you fail or succeed?" *In this failure, what went right?* It's a question people rarely ask about failure "because they're completely focused on what went wrong," says Stanford University's Bob Sutton, author of Scaling Up Excellence. But by paying attention to the small successes within a failure, we're reminded that failure often is not absolute, nor is it an endgame — it is an instructive stage, and one step on a longer journey.

I would also add the question, "What does failure look like in this scenario?" Often, what we think is a failure may even be judged as success by others. Our worst fears might not even be that bad.

When I was at the insurance company, I had been preparing a business case for a new product extension. We felt this product was vital to our success in selling an existing product but also in diversifying our revenue. We had a sound business case and had already sold the idea to our local CEO. I was working closely with the CFO to refine the business case in preparation for our final approval, when I realized I had a formula error in a key spreadsheet — an error that hurt the case. I remember feeling sick as I came to that realization on the phone with the CFO. I was wrecked with thoughts of this being a career-limiting situation for me personally, not to mention a possible loss of credibility for our entire division.

As I began to talk it through, the CFO allayed my fears by letting me in on the fact that this now-lower return was still much higher than the target return he and other executives expected. This potential deep fear was actually nothing to worry about at all.

The process of contemplating failure can be really powerful by forcing you to spend even a few minutes being honest with yourself. It almost never happens in a corporate context. Managers who have early initial success are rewarded with more until they begin to think that failure would never happen to them. Failure will happen, though, and asking questions about what it looks like will help keep managers humble with their success and better able to handle failure when it does occur. This process can help level out the emotional peaks and valleys of the individual successes and failures. Over time, it even trains behaviors to be rooted in reality rather than the false emotions of a fearful moment.

Lean Into Failure for Better Decisions

These questions and exercises are important not only to help us psychologically prepare for failure and bounce back stronger, but also because our bodies need failure to help us grow.

In *Creativity Inc.*, Ed Catmull writes about his view of fear. "My goal is not to drive fear out completely, because fear is inevitable in high-stakes situations. What I want to do is loosen its grip on us. While we don't want too many failures, we must think of the cost of failure as an investment in the future."

Stop and take that thought in for a minute. How much

more bravely would we approach all decisions if our fundamental thought processes included viewing failure as an investment in the future?

Researchers at Johns Hopkins University, as noted in a *Co.Create* article, recently discovered that our ability to perform a physical athletic or creative task isn't entirely about what the body has learned to do right. Instead, we owe our success to the hundred times we've tried to master a skill and failed. "When you're just starting to learn something new, the errors that you experience are helping you learn faster," said David Herzfeld, a PhD student in Biomedical Engineering involved with the Hopkins study.

The researchers used a video game and minor adjustments in the response of the joystick to prove this hypothesis. The scientists secretly reprogrammed the joystick to always send the cursor 30 degrees to the left. After a few huge errors, subjects again adjusted to the new paradigm, learning to aim right. But as soon as they'd gotten the hang of it, the scientists switched the cursor back to its original straight-ahead position. Subjects were again forced to correct their shots, this time by aiming left. The scientists discovered that most people increased the speed at which they were able to readjust.

"We found that if you put people in a situation where the joystick was rotated in a way they'd never seen before, they will learn that faster than a person off the street," said Herzfeld. They were experiencing what Herzfeld calls "savings." It's the idea that you might be a bit rusty after a week-long break from your music practice or your sketch book, but, in a short amount of time, you'll not only meet your previous learning threshold. You'll surpass it. "Every time you get a little faster,"

Herzfeld said, but not simply because your body "remembers" the correct motions. "You're not only recalling the actions that you performed" — the muscle memory — "but you now have a memory of your errors. Such that you can generalize the corrections from those actions to completely new things."

In *Psychology Today*, Dr. Judith Sills writes:

> There's a lot of talk, and a lot to be said, for the power of Yes. Yes supports risk-taking, courage, and an open-hearted approach to life whose grace cannot be minimized. But no — a metal grate that slams shut the window between one's self and the influence of others — is rarely celebrated. It's a hidden power because it is both easily misunderstood and difficult to engage.

The difficult part of no is deciphering when your no comes from a place of fear versus wisdom. Wisdom to know that a particular approach will not lead to success or potentially even be damaging. The inverse is asking yourself if the inclination to say no is a response to an impulse or urge you feel inside you that is based in fear.

Reprogramming Fear Itself

"The only thing we have to fear is fear itself."

— Franklin D. Roosevelt

Up to this point in this book we have outlined a lot of possible fears in a business context, but that is only one type of fear we have to work around. There are really two components of fear in decision-making. One, situational influences of fear. Two, personal fears.

The largest portion of this book has provided the context for the first. Those influences can include Legal, Risk Management, Marketing, Internal Audit, and Corporate Communications departments. But we can't ignore our personal fears as they relate to decision-making.

When we encounter a risky situation, our brains become vulnerable to a process that psychologist Daniel Goleman refers to in a *Fast Company* article as "amygdala hijack." The amygdala — the part of your brain associated with memory, decision-making, and emotional responses — has a quicker reaction time than the cortex, the rational-thinking part of your brain. It's what sends us into fight-or-flight mode. But if we're stressed rather than in real danger, the amygdala can overfire, leading us to make bad decisions:

> When we're stressed the part of the brain that takes
> over, the part that reacts the most, is the circuitry
> that was originally designed to manage threats —
> especially circuits that center on the amygdala. It is
> important to understand that the impulses that come
> to us when we're under stress — particularly if we get
> hijacked by it — are likely to lead us astray.

Let's go back to Chapter 1 and our description of the warrior brain. We talked about how the military attempts to identify and condition how our minds respond to stressful or fearful situations. That assessment forms a significant basis for whether soldiers are selected for special operations teams and in what roles. But there are situations, as described in a Readers

Digest article, where traumatic experiences short-circuit the ability to make decisions with the warrior brain mentality:

> "There are people who make a negative loop about the situation they are placed in," says Potterat. "Those are people who can't cope." It's the people who take control of stressful challenges "in any environment," he says, who will eventually wear the SEAL uniform.

It doesn't have to end there. While some brains are naturally more resistant to stress than others, recent research on Marines diagnosed with PTSD suggests that vulnerable and even traumatized brains can be trained to manage fear more effectively. Martin Paulus, a psychiatrist who has studied the optimal stress responses in SEALs and elite athletes, wondered if resilience was akin to a muscle in the brain that, like all muscles, could be strengthened. "People who have resiliency respond to stressful events in a positive way," he said.

Paulus developed a mental fitness program for a test group of 20 Marine combat veterans with damaged stress responses. Rather than trying to blunt the fears they carried from their battlefield experiences, Paulus intentionally stressed them, restricting their breathing and showing them unpleasant images — like close-ups of angry faces — while observing their brain functions with a scanner.

He likens this to testing knee reflexes with a hammer. The only way to test the fear system is to swing the hammer and apply some stress. Paulus makes the combat vets uncomfortable to help them relearn that anxiety does not equal mortal danger: "The big issue with PTSD is that the brain still links up strong emotional responses to that experience of battle, triggering a cascade of stress responses that were helpful in battle but not now, in real life."

This concept has been taken a step further. A new virtual reality technology called Bravemind even allows the therapy to include a virtual reality simulation. It's all part of an attempt to treat military patients using a technique called "exposure therapy," which conventionally consists of therapists talking their patients through guided encounters with environments like crowded marketplaces, automobiles, and indoor spaces where their initial trauma took place. Therapists want to see if virtually reliving the worst of war can be beneficial for veterans.

After initial brain scans showed the Marines "over responding" to the negative images and other stressors, Paulus put them through an eight-week mindfulness course. The program included "refocusing exercises" in which the vets were taught to mentally recast their traumatic battlefield memories and treat them simply as feelings or as obstacles to overcome. They also learned controlled breathing, meditation, and other relaxation techniques.

Early results from follow-up testing and scans point to improved resiliency among the Marines — or something closer to the warrior brain response, with a less reactive stress circuit and more control from the cognitive part of the brain.

If the concept of stressing in a controlled environment, providing reconditioning exercises, and building resilience and better decision-making can work for the military and veterans, why can't the same concept be applied to a business context?

Re-creating a roadside bomb might not help you during a corporate crisis, but there are business situations that could be simulated to improve decision-making. Based on my experience, one of the few ways where this has been performed regularly to successful outcomes is in Disaster Recovery and Business Continuity tests. We can use this very concept to simulate corporate crises such as a reputation-killing media story, a regulatory action, a class-action lawsuit, or a potentially game-changing product from a competitor.

It is not uncommon for role-playing to be a part of some corporate training programs, including management training courses. But these training programs are rarely taken seriously. I believe a big reason is that the appropriate vision for the training hasn't been cast by senior management.

They are primarily used as an evaluation tool, only secondarily as a coaching or teaching tool. Instead, executives should have a stated goal to build resilient managers able to handle crisis situations with good decision-making. Then, if they follow up with consistent training around the practice scenarios, the program would be much more effective — not just for improving particular decisions, but for improving how managers handle fear in general.

No one questions the training received by the military. They have a clear understanding that they are training for situations they may never encounter, but they understand the purpose of not just knowing how to deal with a situation but also being able to manage your emotions in it. When decisions need to be made in the midst of possibly very bleak circumstances, there's no substitute for training.

Business circumstances might not be nearly as dire as military ones, but the principle still applies. Fear can only truly be overcome in advance. Bravery takes practice.

CONCLUSION

In his book *Between Two Worlds: How the English Became Americans*, Malcolm Gaskill describes the bravery of the early colonists:

> Failing to retain a recognizably English identity caused anxiety and disappointment. But from failure emerged something truly striking, a spirit that resonates in America across the centuries. Colonial character was driven by a creative tension between lofty ideals and mundane desires. Trying to remain the same, it turned out, demanded a constant effort of industry and reinvention.

> Still, for all their diversity and contradictions, English migrants to America tended to conform to a single recognizable type: the intrepid, resilient, undaunted pioneer. In every colony, similar challenges were met with the same determination and optimism.

When we talk about organizational culture, we often talk about it as a recipe. Sprinkle in a little of this, add a dash of that, sift, stir and bake. The colonists remind us that it isn't always what we try to put in, but what we are vigilant to keep out. How we respond to our surrounding circumstances can define us.

We clearly need to create a culture that promotes sensible risk-taking, encourages individuality, and allows people to operate in the fullness of their strengths. But we can't lose sight of the fact that many of our employees — much like the pilgrims trying to recreate England — are just trying to create an environment that allows them to provide financially for their families. Given the right environment that challenges without punishing for losses, a group of people can emerge with a culture that doesn't include fear as a motivator.

Your employees will own this culture because it is theirs. It is influenced by each of them in some small way. They identify with it, so it is natural. It's often hard to identify exactly what recipe makes a culture what it is, but one thing is never an ingredient: fear.

To use one last sports example, think of historically great teams — the San Francisco 49ers in the 80s, the Chicago Bulls in the 90s, the New York Yankees in early 2000s. These teams have no real common cultural connections, but they were each confident in their moment and not motivated by fear.

John Michael, a leadership expert who spent decades commanding the US Air Force, outlines four impacts of fear:

Fear influences us in a variety of ways. It makes us more *judgmental,* leading us to impute negative motivations to others' innocent actions. Fear makes us more *pessimistic*, leading us to develop a sense of helplessness about our ability to deal with life's challenges. It increases our *pessimism*, convincing us to believe that the future is bleak. And perhaps above all, fear leads to develop an *aversion to risk-taking*. It convinces us to play it safe and lead lives far smaller than we are capable of living.

Fear is limiting. It is content with living small, constrained and underwhelmed. Fear doesn't accomplish. It defeats. Fear plays the short game. It masquerades as momentary success, but then, once it has infected your culture, it destroys you in the long run.

I've spent a lot of time in this book outlining specific people, events, and behaviors that lead to fear. I've talked about many negative consequences of responding irrationally to the emotions that we conjure.

But now, to sum up why fear matters so much — and why it matters so much to build capabilities that slow our heart rate long enough to process fears and respond accordingly — I want simply to remember the fate of the whaleship *Essex*: a boat destroyed, its individuals defeated, all of their potential sinking into the ocean.

The same thing is happening in our business organizations because of the foothold fear has been given and in place of a destroyed boat we have unproductive businesses, in place of defeated individuals we have disengaged employees and in place of sinking potential we have lost cultures that communicate sinking potential to employees, customers and investors.

Many organizations will plod along hoping a new product

will come along and put some pop back into revenue growth or that the new software implementation will provide dramatic improvements in customer service or any number of other initiatives will be the silver bullet. And strategy is important but with a cultural rot simmering beneath the surface hope is lost.

However, this doesn't have to be your organization's fate. Eradicating fear should be your most important business goal. By addressing the eight fear factors and restoring your organization's core and improving decision making you will release your employees to provide that creative spark you need to enhance revenue, gain buy-in on that big process transformation, improve customer satisfaction and most importantly build a thriving organization that is ready to excel in the next decade, not just the next quarter.

Sources and References By chapter, in order of appearance.

Introduction

New International Version Bible. Zondervan, 1978.

Walker, Karen Thompson. "What Fear Can Teach Us." TED Talks. Speech. June 1, 2012.

Philbrick, Nathaniel. *In the Heart of the Sea: The Tragedy of the Whaleship* Essex. New York: Viking, 2000.

Chapter 1

"Fear." *Definitions.net*. Accessed April 4, 2015.

Bradberry, Travis, and Jean Greaves. *Emotional Intelligence 2.0*.

Davey, GCL eds. (1997) *Phobias: A handbook of theory, research and treatment*. Wiley, Chichester, pp. 301-322

Field, Andy P. "The Behavioral Inhibition System and the Verbal Information Pathway to Children's Fears." *Journal of Abnormal Psychology*: 742-52.

New International Version Bible. Zondervan, 1978.

Wallace, Kathryn. "How the Science of Fear Makes Soldiers Stronger." *Reader's Digest*. January 31, 2013.

Chapter 2

Hadfield, Chris. "What I Learned from Going Blind in Space." *TED Talks*. Speech. March 1, 2014.

Godin, Seth. "Our Crystal Palace." *Seth's Blog*. October 23, 2013.

Russell, James S. "World Trade Center Bosses Turn Site into Grim Fortress." *Bloomberg Business*. July 25, 2013.

Campanile, Carl. "Bloomberg to Urge Cuomo to Veto Bill to Allow Sparkler Sales outside of NYC over Terror Target Fears." *New York Post*. June 26, 2013.

Winter, Michael. "Sales of Armored Backpacks for Kids Soar." *USA Today*. December 19, 2012.

Cloud, John. "Hardwire's Armored Whiteboards Defend Against School Shootings." *Bloomberg Business*. October 2, 2014.

Britt, Robert. "The Odds of Dying." *LiveScience*. January 6, 2005.

Housel, Morgan. "Why We're Awful at Assessing Risk." *The Motley Fool*. March 14, 2014.

"The Feelings In Facebook Status Updates Are Contagious And Spread Like A Virus." Co.Exist, *Fast Company*. March 12, 2014.

Story, Louise. "Anywhere the Eye Can See, It's Likely to See an Ad." *The New York Times*. January 14, 2007.

Honan, Mat. "I Liked Everything I Saw on Facebook for Two Days. Here's What It Did to Me." *Wired*. August 11, 2014.

Beer, Jeff. "Now That's Getting Them Early: Mitsubishi Gives Newborns Their First Ride Home." *Fast Company*. April 9, 2014.

Pearson, Bryan. "From Selling Beauty to Selling Fear." *The Conference Board Review*. 2012.

Mahapatra, Lisa. "How the Average United States Resident Spends Time." *International Business Times*. Infographic. 2013.

"Five Years after Lehman, World Is Hoarding Cash." *CNBC*. October 6, 2013.

Saporito, Bill. "Sin City Meets the Low Rollers." *Time*. August 19, 2013.

"Household Debt and Disposable Income." Federal Reserve Board, Haver Analytics. Chart. 2010.

"National Consumer Financial Literacy Survey Results for 2013." Inceptia Institute. 2013.

Chapter 3

Kluger, Jeffrey. "The Happiness of Pursuit." *Time*. July 8, 2013.

Hathaway, Ian, and Robert E. Litan. "Declining Business Dynamism in the United States: A Look at States and Metros." *Brookings*. The Brookings Institution. May 5, 2014.

Ingraham, Christopher. "U.S. Businesses Are Being Destroyed Faster than They're Being Created." *Washington Post*. May 5, 2014.

Simon, Ruth, and Caelainn Barr. "Endangered Species: Young U.S. Entrepreneurs." *The Wall Street Journal*. January 2, 2015.

Xavier, Siri Roland, Donna Kelley, et al. *GEM 2012 Global Report*. Global Entrepreneurship Monitor. Jan 2013.

New International Version Bible. Zondervan, 1978.

Lee, Timothy B. "The IPO Is Dying. Marc Andreessen Explains Why." *Vox*. June 26, 2014.

Lewis, Michael. "The Wolf Hunters of Wall Street." *The New York Times*. April 5, 2014.

"The Big Engine That Couldn't." *The Economist*. May 19, 2012.

Upbin, Bruce. "The Six Habits Of Successful Private Companies." *Forbes*. June 30, 2013.

Summers, Nick. "IBM's EPS Target Unhelpful Amid Cloud Computing Challenges." *Bloomberg Business*. May 22, 2014.

Chapter 4

Smith, Jeremy Adam. "Learning to Trust Each Other, Online and Off." *Shareable*. October 12, 2010.

Green, Jeff. "Jumbo Severance Packages for Top CEOs Are Growing." *Bloomberg Business*. June 6, 2013.

Sacks, Danielle. "10 Creativity Tips From J.Crew CEO Mickey Drexler." *Fast Company*. April 15, 2013.

Lazonick, William. "Profits Without Prosperity." *Harvard Business Review*. September 1, 2014.

"State of the American Workplace." *Gallup*. 2013.

Anderson, Cameron, and Courtney E. Brown. "The Functions And Dysfunctions Of Hierarchy." *Research in Organizational Behavior*, 2010.

Haden, Jeff. "Why There Are No Job Titles at My Company." *Inc.com*. October 1, 2013.

Brown, Brené. *Daring Greatly: How the Courage to Be Vulnerable Transforms the Way We Live, Love, Parent, and Lead*. New York, NY: Gotham Books, 2012.

Bodell, LIsa and Ron Ashkenas. "The Reason Your Team Won't Take Risks." *Harvard Business Review*. September 9, 2014.

McWhinnie, Eric. "Wall Street Is Awash in Cash." *USA Today*. April 20, 2014.

Ritchie, James. "Do You Really Have a Strategy? Here's What P&G's A.G. Lafley Thinks." *The Business Journals*. January 30, 2013.

Brunstein, Joachim C., and Peter M. Gollwitzer. "Effects of

Failure on Subsequent Performance: The Importance
of Self-defining Goals." *Journal of Personality and Social
Psychology*: 395-407.

Rowling, J.K. "The Fringe Benefits of Failure, and the
Importance of Imagination." Speech. June 5, 2008.

Sacks, Danielle. "How Jenna Lyons Transformed J.Crew Into
A Cult Brand." *Fast Company*. April 15, 2013.

McCracken, Harry. "Google vs. Death." *Time*. September 30,
2013.

Philbrick, Nathaniel. *In the Heart of the Sea: The Tragedy of the
Whaleship* Essex. New York: Viking, 2000.

Chapter 5

Kolhatkar, Sheelah. "Lynn Tilton on Reviving MD
Helicopters and U.S. Manufacturing." *Bloomberg Business*.
August 8, 2013.

Matuson, Roberta. "Uncovering Talent: A New Model For
Inclusion And Diversity." *Fast Company*. September 11,
2013.

Zenger, Jack, and Joseph Folkman. "Your Employees Want
the Negative Feedback You Hate to Give." *Harvard
Business Review*. January 15, 2014.

Nickish, Curt. "Is It Time To Get Rid Of Noncompete
Agreements?" *Here & Now*. Radio show. WBUR Boston.
July 7, 2014.

Cowherd, Colin. *The Herd*. Radio show. ESPN Radio. 2014.

Doyel, Gregg. "Carroll's Vision in '12 Preseason Put Wilson
at QB, Helped Seattle to SB." *CBSSports.com*. January 29,
2014.

Philbrick, Nathaniel. *In the Heart of the Sea: The Tragedy of the
Whaleship* Essex. New York: Viking, 2000.

Chapter 6

Whipple, Edwin Percy. *American Literature, and Other Papers.* Boston: Ticknor and Company, 1887.

Renzo, Lucioni. "United States of Amoeba." *The Economist.* December 7, 2013. Infographic.

Welch, Jack and Suzy. "Schmooze or Lose: How the Lost Art of Negotiation Led to a Shutdown." *LinkedIn.* October 2, 2013.

Schmidt, Robert. "SEC Employees Get Union Warning About Lunch Limit." *Bloomberg Business.* November 7, 2013.

Klein, Joe. "Can Service Save Us? " *Time.* June 20, 2013.

Gratton, Lynda. "Leading in Complex Times." *Harvard Business Review.* October 21, 2013.

Philbrick, Nathaniel. *In the Heart of the Sea: The Tragedy of the Whaleship* Essex. New York: Viking, 2000.

Chapter 7

"Cold Warriors: Wolves and Buffalo." *Nature.* TV Show. February 13, 2013.

Goldberg, David. "What You Can Learn From My Rookie Mistakes." *LinkedIn.* August 5, 2013.

Krasny, Jill. "Why Competition May Be the Best Thing for Your Business." *Inc.com.* November 1, 2013.

Stone, Brad. *The Everything Store: Jeff Bezos and the Age of Amazon.* Little, Brown, and Company, 2013.

Treacy, Michael, and Frederik D. Wiersema. *The Discipline of Market Leaders: Choose Your Customers, Narrow Your Focus, Dominate Your Market.* Reading, Mass.: Addison-Wesley Pub., 1995.

"Economic Moat Definition | Investopedia." *Investopedia.* November 17, 2003. Accessed February 9, 2015.

Nir, Sarah Maslin. "The Food May Be Fast, but These Customers Won't Be Rushed." *The New York Times.* January 27, 2014.

Musk, Elon. "All Our Patent Are Belong To You." *Tesla Motors Blog*. June 12, 2014.

DeGusta, Michael. "The REAL Death Of The Music Industry." *Business Insider*. February 18, 2011.

Kirsner, Scott. "11 Ways Big Companies Undermine Innovation." *Harvard Business Review*. October 21, 2013.

Carr, Austin, and Mark Wilson. "Facebook's Plan To Own Your Phone." *Fast Company*. June 16, 2014.

Catmull, Edwin E., and Amy Wallace. *Creativity, Inc.: Overcoming the Unseen Forces That Stand in the Way of True Inspiration*. Random House, 2014.

Philbrick, Nathaniel. *In the Heart of the Sea: The Tragedy of the Whaleship* Essex. New York: Viking, 2000.

Chapter 8

"Global Regulatory Activity in the Financial Industry." Thomson Reuters and The Financial Brand. October, 2013. Chart.

"Americans' Overall Perceptions on Government Regulation of Business." *Gallup*. September, 2014. Chart.

Lindsay, Tom. "University Of Texas Looks To Limit Administrative Bloat." *Forbes*. January 24, 2015.

Marcus, Jon. "New Analysis Shows Problematic Boom In Higher Ed Administrators." *The Huffington Post*. February 6, 2014.

"Strengthened but not simplified." *Issues Facing JPM, the Industry, and Global Economy*. JP Morgan Chase & Co. Infographic. September 2010.

Bennett, Drake. "Risk Ahoy: Maersk, Daewoo Build the World's Biggest Boat." *Bloomberg Business*. September 5, 2013.

Calabresi, Massimo. "Bank Oversight For Hire." *Time*. September 23, 2013.

Vara, Vauhini. "How Obamacare Got CVS to Stop Selling Cigarettes." *The New Yorker*. September 4, 2014.

Philbrick, Nathaniel. *In the Heart of the Sea: The Tragedy of the Whaleship* Essex. New York: Viking, 2000.

Chapter 9

Statistical Abstract of the United States. 2012, US Census Bureau.

2013/2014 Global Fraud Report. 2014, Kroll.

Lee, Timothy B. "The IPO Is Dying. Marc Andreessen Explains Why." *Vox.* June 26, 2014.

Sterngold, James. "After Crisis, Risk Officers Gain More Clout at Banks." *The Wall Street Journal.* June 25, 2014.

Osterloh, Margit, and Bruno S. Frey. "Corporate Governance for Crooks? The Case for Corporate Virtue." *SSRN Journal,* 2003.

Sorkin, Andrew Ross. "Berkshire's Radical Strategy: Trust." *The New York Times.* May 5, 2014.

Catmull, Edwin E., and Amy Wallace. *Creativity, Inc.: Overcoming the Unseen Forces That Stand in the Way of True Inspiration.* Random House, 2014.

"Eighty Percent of Chief Audit Executives Acknowledge Room for Improvement with Internal Audit Functions." *Ernst & Young.* July 18, 2012.

"SJ (Protector) Personality Temperament." *MyPersonality.info.* Accessed March 12, 2015.

Sutherland, Rory. "Life lessons from an ad man." *TED Talks.* Speech. July 2009.

Sterngold, James. Ibid.

Pulse of the Profession. 2012, *Institute of Internal Auditors.*

Philbrick, Nathaniel. *In the Heart of the Sea: The Tragedy of the Whaleship* Essex. New York: Viking, 2000.

Chapter 10

Woolner, Ann, and Felix Gilette. "For Paula Deen, Management Mess Leads to Career Meltdown." *Bloomberg Business.* July 3, 2013.

"Lawfare." Wikipedia, The Free Encyclopedia. Accessed January 7, 2015.

Barrett, Paul M. "Mass Tort Lawsuit Lead Generator Jesse Levine Has Victims for Sale." *Bloomberg Business.* December 12, 2013.

Decker, Susan. "A Cheaper Way to Defuse Patent Claims: Kill the Patent" *Bloomberg Business.* October 24, 2013.

"Effect of Patent Troll Lawsuits on Innovation." *Harvard Business Review.* 2014. Chart.

Mullin, Joe. "FindTheBest Destroys "matchmaking" Patent, Pushes RICO Case against Troll." *Ars Technica.* November 23, 2013.

"What do you call 176,000 lawyers lying at the bottom of the ocean?" *Bloomberg Business.* May 6, 2013.

Fulbright's 9th Annual Litigation Trends. Norton Rose Fulbright. February, 2013.

"Litigious America." *Newsweek.* July, 2001.

Barrett, Paul M. "Toyota Accelerator Lawsuits Keep Coming." *Bloomberg Business.* November 7, 2013.

Woolner, Ann, and Felix Gilette. "For Paula Deen, Management Mess Leads to Career Meltdown." *Bloomberg Business.* July 3, 2013.

Heath, Thomas. "Capital Buzz: Lockheed Martin Makes Changes to Its Compensation Plan." *Washington Post.* February 3, 2013.

Chung, Lauren M. "Top In-House Legal Salaries Are Up, Reflecting Greater CLO Role." *Today's General Counsel.* March 26, 2013.

"A Compelling Case For Lawyer-CEOs." *Bloomberg Business.* December 12, 2004.

Curridan, Mark. "CEO, Esq." *ABA Journal.* May 1, 2010.

O'Reilly, Tim. "How I Failed." *LinkedIn*. September 13, 2013.

Carr, Austin. "Deep Inside Taco Bell's Doritos Locos Taco." *Fast Company*. May 1, 2013.

Sternbergh, Adam. "Book Review: The Firm by Duff McDonald." *Bloomberg Business*. September 5, 2013.

"Replacing the Board." *The Economist*. August 16, 2014.

Hertz, Noreena. "Why We Make Bad Decisions." *The New York Times*. October 19, 2013.

Philbrick, Nathaniel. *In the Heart of the Sea: The Tragedy of the Whaleship* Essex. New York: Viking, 2000.

Chapter 11

Sifferlin, Alice. "Menopausal Muddle." *Time*. August 5, 2013.

Housel, Morgan. "I'm Just Now Realizing How Stupid We Are." *The Motley Fool*. June 11, 2014.

Carter, Bill. "CNN's Ratings Surge Covering the Mystery of the Missing Airliner." *The New York Times*. March 17, 2014.

Musk, Elon. "Model S Fire." *Tesla Motors Blog*. October 4, 2013.

Greenberg, Mike, and Mike Golic. *Mike & Mike Radio Show*. ESPN. Radio. June 2014.

"Apple Playbook." *9to5Mac*. 2015.

"Four big names lose: 36,733 readers rate the food, value, staff, and speed at 53 chains." *Consumer Reports*. August, 2011.

Jargon, Julie. "How to Revive McDonald's? Ideas from Four Experts." *The Wall Street Journal*. December 23, 2014.

Safian, Robert. "Generation Flux's Secret Weapon." Fast Company. November, 2014.

Kurp, Josh. "DiGiorno's Unfortunate Hashtag Is Why Brands Shouldn't Be Allowed To Tweet." *Uproxx*. September 9, 2014.

Shaw, Colin. "What Santa Teaches Us About Making

Customers Believe." *Beyond Philosophy*. December 27, 2013.

Philbrick, Nathaniel. *In the Heart of the Sea: The Tragedy of the Whaleship* Essex. New York: Viking, 2000.

Chapter 12

Hadfield, Chris. "What I Learned from Going Blind in Space." *TED Talks*. Speech. March 1, 2014.

Gillett, Rachel. "What the Hype Behind Embracing Failure Is Really All About." *Fast Company*. September 8, 2014.

Chapter 13

Schwartz, Tony, and Christine Porath. "Why You Hate Work." *The New York Times*. May 31, 2014.

Gavett, Gretchen. "Why a Quarter of Americans Don't Trust Their Employers." *Harvard Business Review*. April 28, 2014.

Jones, Bruce. "How Strategic Is Your Social Media Recruiting? Why You Should D'Think It." *Talking Point: The Disney Institute Blog*. July 8, 2014.

Zook, Chris, and James Allen. *Repeatability: Build Enduring Businesses for a World of Constant Change*. Boston, Mass.: Harvard Business Review Press, 2012.

Wagner, Tony, and Robert A. Compton. *Creating Innovators: The Making of Young People Who Will Change the World*. New York: Scribner, 2012.

"Why Companies Are Terrible At Spotting Creative Ideas." *Co.Design*. Fast Company. December 11, 2013.

Sullivan, John. "Using Job Rotations for Improving Development and Retention." *SlideShare*. November 16, 2009. Presentation.

Zolli, Andrew, and Ann Marie Healy. *Resilience: Why Things Bounce Back*. New York: Free Press, 2012.

Perlis, Margaret. "5 Characteristics Of Grit — How Many Do You Have?" *Forbes*. October 29, 2013.

Stoltz, Paul Gordon. *Grit: The New Science of What It Takes to Persevere, Flourish, Succeed*. Climb Strong Press, 2015.

Chapter 14

Weisenthal, Joe. "BUFFETT: Here's A Message To My Fellow CEOs Who Whine Incessantly About 'Uncertainty'." *Business Insider*. March 1, 2013.

Sinek, Simon. "How Great Leaders Inspire Action." *TED Talks*. Speech. September, 2009.

Feintzeig, Rachel. "You're Awesome! Firms Scrap Negative Feedback." *The Wall Street Journal*. February 10, 2015.

"70/20/10 Model." *Wikipedia*. Wikipedia, The Free Encyclopedia. Accessed March 10, 2015.

de Franciscis, Maurizio. *Capture Your Flag*. Capture Your Flag, LLC. Interview. October 25, 2011.

Rouen, Ethan. "When Leaders Are Scarce, Employees Look to Peers." *Fortune*. April 19, 2012.

Macbride, Elizabeth. "5 Ways Entrepreneurs Sabotage Their Own Media Coverage." *Forbes*. August 13, 2014.

Mathews, Anna Wilde, and Theo Francis. "Aetna Sets Wage Floor: $16 an Hour." *The Wall Street Journal*. January 12, 2015.

Chapter 15

Chang, Ruth. "How to Make Hard Choices." *TED Talks*. Speech. May, 2014.

Ashkenas, Ron. "When an Inability to Make Decisions Is Actually Fear of Conflict." *Harvard Business Review*. June 4, 2014

Berger, Warren. *A More Beautiful Question: The Power of Inquiry to Spark Breakthrough Ideas*. Bloomsbury USA, 2014.

Catmull, Edwin E., and Amy Wallace. *Creativity, Inc.: Overcoming the Unseen Forces That Stand in the Way of True Inspiration*. Random House, 2014.

Miller, Jennifer. "Science Confirms It: If You Want To Succeed, You Have To Screw Up." *Co.Create. Fast Company*. August 24, 2014.

Sills, Judith. "The Power of No." *Psychology Today*. November 5, 2013.

Porter, Jane. "The Connection Between Fear and Career Regret." *Fast Company*. December 1, 2014.

Wallace, Kathryn. "How the Science of Fear Makes Soldiers Stronger." *Reader's Digest*. January 31, 2013.

Soares, J M, A. Sampaio, L M Ferreira, N C Santos, F. Marques, J A Palha, J J Cerqueira, and N. Sousa. "Stress-induced Changes in Human Decision-making Are Reversible." *Translational Psychiatry*: E131.

Conclusion

Malcolm, Gaskill. *Between Two Worlds: How the English Became Americans*. Oxford University Press, 2014.

Michael, John. "Fear Factor." *LinkedIn*. January 18, 2015.

CPSIA information can be obtained
at www.ICGtesting.com
Printed in the USA
FFOW05n1316230915

9 780692 492291